陈琳云

P9-CEU-772

MASTERMINDS Riddle Math Series

GEOMETRY AND GRAPHING

Reproducible Skill Builders And Higher Order Thinking Activities Based On NCTM Standards

By Brenda Opie, Lory Jackson,
Douglas McAvinn, and Nancy Ygnve

Incentive Publications, Inc.
Nashville, Tennessee

Illustrated by Douglas McAvinn
Cover illustration by Douglas McAvinn

ISBN 0-86530-305-3

Copyright ©1995 by Incentive Publications, Inc., Nashville, TN. All rights reserved. No part of this publication may be reproduced, stored in a retrieval system, or transmitted in any form or by any means (electronic, mechanical, photocopying, recording, or otherwise) without written permission from Incentive Publications, Inc., with the exception below.

Pages labeled with the statement ©1995 by Incentive Publications, Inc., Nashville, TN are intended for reproduction. Permission is hereby granted to the purchaser of one copy of GEOMETRY AND GRAPHING to reproduce these pages in sufficient quantities for meeting the purchaser's own classroom needs.

PRINTED IN THE UNITED STATES OF AMERICA

TABLE OF CONTENTS

NAME_____

Why did Mickey Mouse go into outer space?

DIRECTIONS: First, complete each definition below with one of the answers listed at the bottom of the page. Then, write the letter of the definition above the correct answer.

D = A part of a line that begins at an endpoint and goes forever in one direction is a _____

F = A polygon with four sides is a _____

L = An instrument used to measure angles is a _____

N = An angle that measures 90° is a _____ angle

O = The common endpoint of the sides of an angle is called a _____

U = A triangle with no congruent sides is a _____ triangle

I = Lines that meet or cross at one point are called _____ lines

O = An angle that measures more than 90° but less than 180° is an _____ angle

T = The distance around a polygon - the sum of the lengths of its sides is called the _____

P = Lines that never meet are _____ lines

T = A five-sided polygon is a _____

Pentagon	Vertex	Quadrilateral	Intersecting	Right	Ray	Parallel	Protractor	Scalene	Perimeter	Obtuse

©1995 by Incentive Publications, Inc., Nashville, TN.

Applying geometry in our daily lives   NAME_____

Lines, Rays, and Line Segments

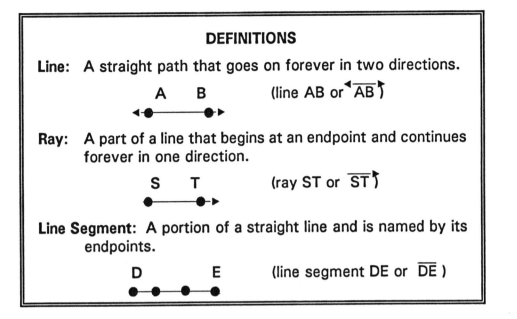

DEFINITIONS

Line: A straight path that goes on forever in two directions.

A   B   (line AB or $\overleftrightarrow{AB}$)

Ray: A part of a line that begins at an endpoint and continues forever in one direction.

S   T   (ray ST or $\overrightarrow{ST}$)

Line Segment: A portion of a straight line and is named by its endpoints.

D   E   (line segment DE or $\overline{DE}$)

DIRECTIONS: Give three or more examples of how each of the above geometric terms can be used to represent measurement in our lives. An example has been done for you in each category.

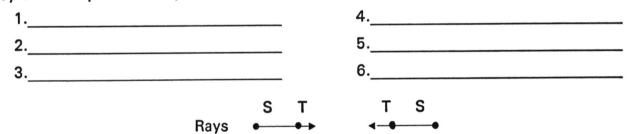

A   B
Lines ◄•————•►

Example: The total number of stars in our universe. (There is an infinite number of stars; therefore, they can be represented by a line.)

1._____   4._____

2._____   5._____

3._____   6._____

S   T   T   S
Rays •——•►   ◄•——•

Example: The light from a flashlight. (You know the origin of the light, but you cannot measure exactly the distance the light travels.)

1._____   4._____

2._____   5._____

3._____   6._____

D   E
Line Segments •——•

Example: The measurement of the length of your math book.

1._____   4._____

2._____   5._____

3._____   6._____

©1995 by Incentive Publications, Inc., Nashville, TN.

Changing Line Segments

DIRECTIONS: Using the dot pattern given below, draw four line segments <u>without</u> retracing or lifting your pencil off the paper so that each of the points shown is on at least one of the segments. You have two sets of dots with which to achieve this challenge. (You can always draw your own dots on another sheet of paper.)

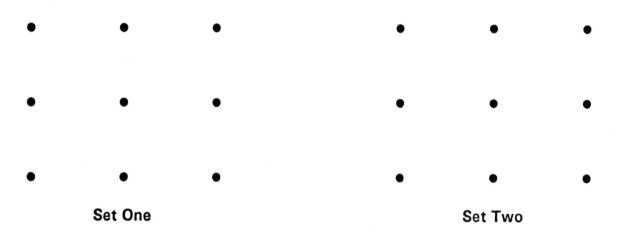

Set One   Set Two

DIRECTIONS: There is an infinite number of lines which can be drawn through one point.

Example:

Exactly one line can be drawn through 2 points.

How many lines can be drawn through the points in each figure below? (assuming no three points are collinear*)

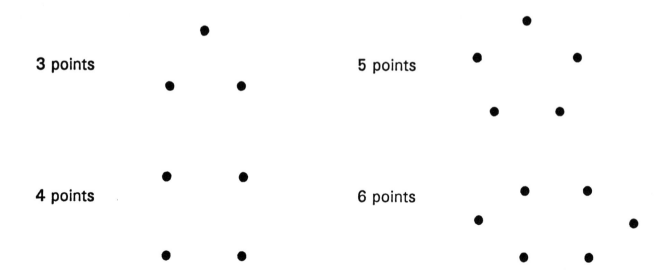

3 points

5 points

4 points

6 points

*Collinear - Points all in one line

©1995 by Incentive Publications, Inc., Nashville, TN.

Solving problems involving angles

NAME _____

When Adam introduced himself to Eve, what three words did he use which are the same when read forwards or backwards?

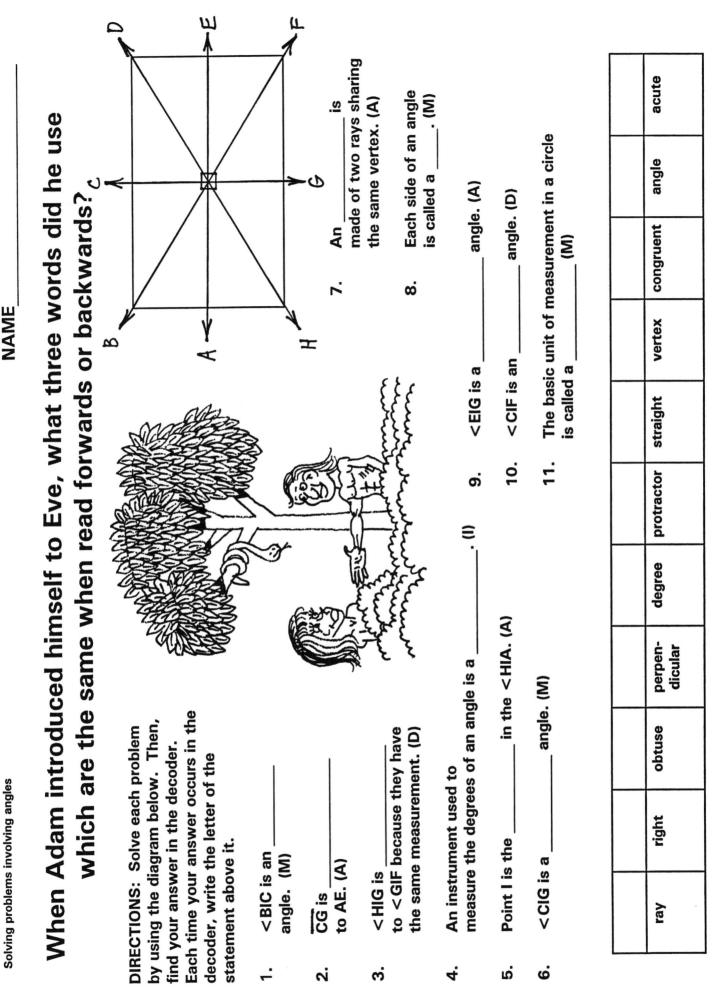

DIRECTIONS: Solve each problem by using the diagram below. Then, find your answer in the decoder. Each time your answer occurs in the decoder, write the letter of the statement above it.

1. <BIC is an _____ angle. (M)

2. $\overline{CG}$ is _____ to AE. (A)

3. <HIG is _____ to <GIF because they have the same measurement. (D)

4. An instrument used to measure the degrees of an angle is a _____. (I)

5. Point I is the _____ in the <HIA. (A)

6. <CIG is a _____ angle. (M)

7. An _____ is made of two rays sharing the same vertex. (A)

8. Each side of an angle is called a _____. (M)

9. <EIG is a _____ angle. (A)

10. <CIF is an _____ angle. (D)

11. The basic unit of measurement in a circle is called a _____ (M)

right	obtuse	perpen-dicular	degree	protractor	straight	vertex	congruent	angle	acute
ray									

©1995 by Incentive Publications, Inc., Nashville, TN.

NAME_____

What is the title of this picture?

DIRECTIONS: Measure the degrees in each angle drawn below. Find your answer in the secret code. Each time your answer appears in the secret code, write the letter of the problem above it.

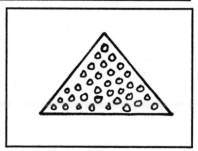

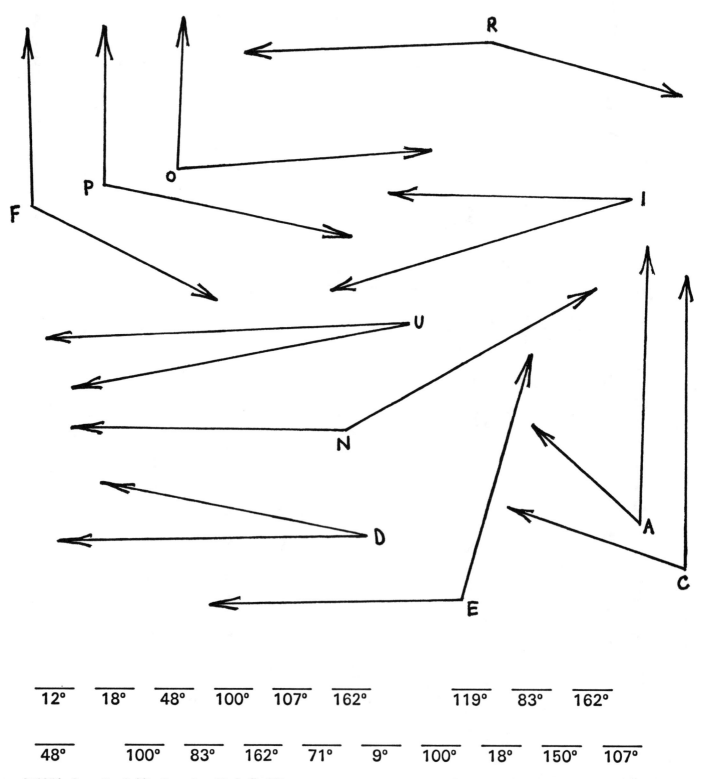

$\overline{\quad\quad}$ $\overline{\quad\quad}$ $\overline{\quad\quad}$ $\overline{\quad\quad}$ $\overline{\quad\quad}$ $\overline{\quad\quad}$ $\overline{\quad\quad}$ $\overline{\quad\quad}$ $\overline{\quad\quad}$
  12°   18°   48°   100°   107°   162°   119°   83°   162°

$\overline{\quad\quad}$ $\overline{\quad\quad}$ $\overline{\quad\quad}$ $\overline{\quad\quad}$ $\overline{\quad\quad}$ $\overline{\quad\quad}$ $\overline{\quad\quad}$ $\overline{\quad\quad}$ $\overline{\quad\quad}$ $\overline{\quad\quad}$
  48°   100°   83°   162°   71°   9°   100°   18°   150°   107°

©1995 by Incentive Publications, Inc., Nashville, TN.

Measuring the degrees in angles

What does the runner-up in a "Miss Universe" contest win?

DIRECTIONS: Measure the degrees in each of the angles drawn below. Find your answer in the secret code at the bottom of the page. Each time your answers appears in the secret code, write the letter of the problem above it.

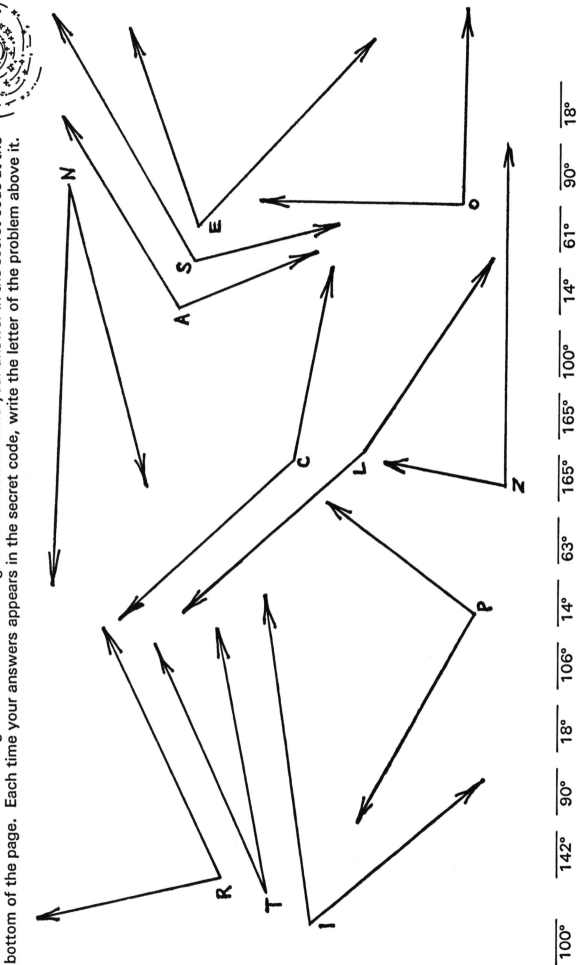

100°	142°	90°	18°	106°	14°	63°	165°	165°	100°	14°	61°	90°	18°

95°	76°	61°	81°	63°

©1995 by Incentive Publications, Inc., Nashville, TN.

TRIANGLE MANIA

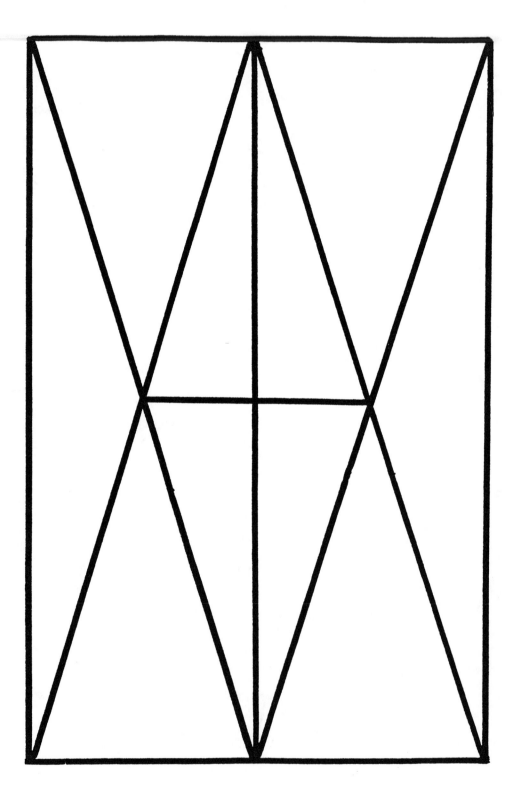

How many triangles can you count?_____

©1995 by Incentive Publications, Inc. Nashville TN

Recognizing acute, obtuse and right angles

NAME _____

What's Dracula's favorite coffee?

DIRECTIONS: Answer each question below and then find your answer in the decoder at the bottom of the page. Each time your answer occurs in the decoder, write the letter of the problem above it.

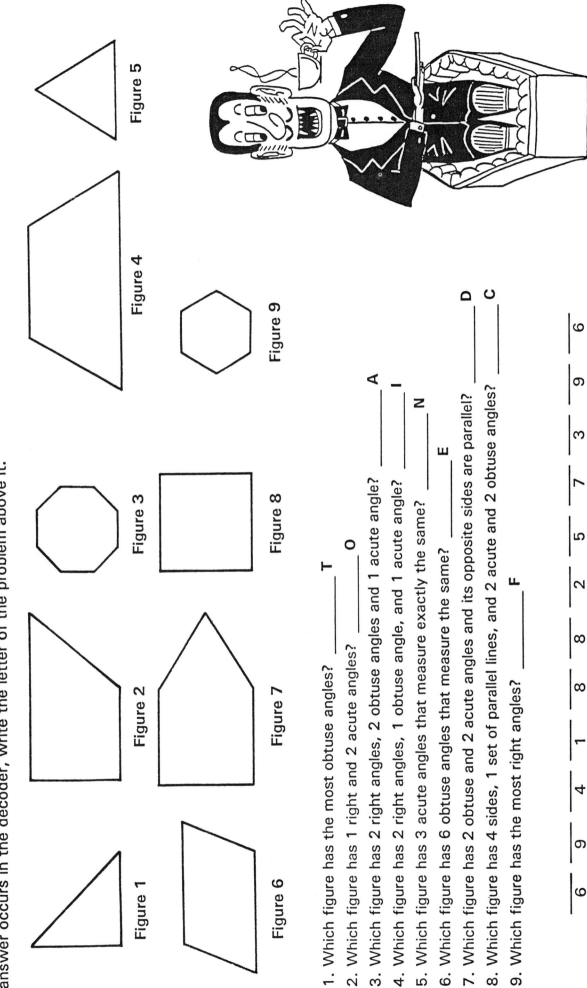

Figure 5

Figure 4

Figure 9

Figure 3

Figure 8

Figure 1

Figure 2

Figure 7

Figure 6

1. Which figure has the most obtuse angles? _____ T

2. Which figure has 1 right and 2 acute angles? _____ O

3. Which figure has 2 right angles, 2 obtuse angles and 1 acute angle? _____ A

4. Which figure has 2 right angles, 1 obtuse angle, and 1 acute angle? _____ I

5. Which figure has 3 acute angles that measure exactly the same? _____ N

6. Which figure has 6 obtuse angles that measure the same? _____ E

7. Which figure has 2 obtuse and 2 acute angles and its opposite sides are parallel? _____ D

8. Which figure has 4 sides, 1 set of parallel lines, and 2 acute and 2 obtuse angles? _____ C

9. Which figure has the most right angles? _____ F

___ ___ ___ ___ ___ ___ ___ ___ ___ ___
6 9 4 1 8 8 2 5 7 3 9 6

©1995 by Incentive Publications, Inc., Nashville, TN.

NAME_____

Why should you beware of your computer?

DIRECTIONS: Answer each question below with the number of the polygon, then find your answer in the decoder at the bottom of the page. Each time your answer occurs in the decoder, write the letter of the problem above it.

Which polygon is a

1. triangle with 3 congruent angles and 3 congruent sides? _____ **C**

2. quadrilateral with 4 congruent sides and no right angles? _____ **U**

3. quadrilateral whose opposite sides are parallel and of equal length? _____ **A**

4. rectangle that has equal sides? _____ **S**

5. quadrilateral that has exactly one pair of parallel sides? _____ **B**

6. triangle with exactly two congruent sides and two congruent angles? _____ **T**

7. triangle with no congruent sides and no congruent angles? _____ **E**

8. quadrilateral with four right angles and opposite sides are congruent? _____ **I**

9. a polygon with five sides? _____ **Y**

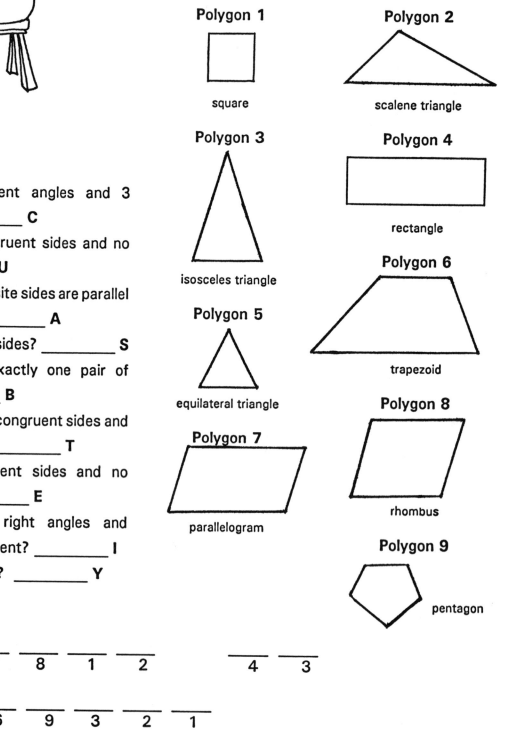

Polygon 1

square

Polygon 2

scalene triangle

Polygon 3

isosceles triangle

Polygon 4

rectangle

Polygon 5

equilateral triangle

Polygon 6

trapezoid

Polygon 7

parallelogram

Polygon 8

rhombus

Polygon 9

pentagon

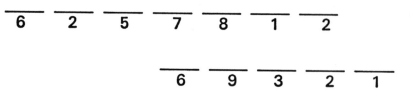

$\overline{\quad}_{6} \ \overline{\quad}_{2} \ \overline{\quad}_{5} \ \overline{\quad}_{7} \ \overline{\quad}_{8} \ \overline{\quad}_{1} \ \overline{\quad}_{2} \qquad \overline{\quad}_{4} \ \overline{\quad}_{3}$

$\overline{\quad}_{6} \ \overline{\quad}_{9} \ \overline{\quad}_{3} \ \overline{\quad}_{2} \ \overline{\quad}_{1}$

©1995 by Incentive Publications, Inc., Nashville, TN.

Designing with geometric figures

NAME_____

Geobot

DIRECTIONS: Design a robot that is made of many different geometric figures (Geobot).

The many different figures I used to create my geobot are:

_____ _____ _____

_____ _____ _____

_____ _____ _____

_____ _____ _____

Write one paragraph telling why your geobot is special and what kinds of things it can do.

_____

_____

_____

_____

_____

_____

_____

_____

_____

©1995 by Incentive Publications, Inc., Nashville, TN.

NAME_____

What do you call an attractive angle?

DIRECTIONS: Using the figure below, complete the following statements with one of the answers given at the bottom of the page. Then, write the letter of the statement above the correct answer.

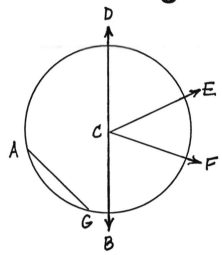

1.   <DCE is an _____ angle. (N)

2.   A circle is composed of _____ degrees. (U)

3. $\overline{BC}$ is a _____ because it is one-half of a diameter. (T)

4.   Any part of a circle such as exists between point D and point E is called an _____. (E)

5.   AG is a _____. (G)

6. $\overline{DB}$ is a _____. (L)

7.   <ECB is an _____ angle. (A)

8.   The distance around a circle is called the _____. (C)

9.   <DCB is a _____ angle. (N)

10.   <ECF measures _____ degrees. (E)

11.   If $\overline{DB}$ measures 12 cm, then $\overline{DC}$ should measure _____cm. (A)

12.   <DCF measures _____ degrees. (A)

6	acute	110	circumference	360	radius	43	obtuse	straight	chord	diameter	arc

©1995 by Incentive Publications, Inc., Nashville, TN

NAME _____

Using geometry in our daily lives

Geometry In Our Environment

DIRECTIONS: Find examples in your environment of the following geometric figures and then illustrate in the boxes below how each of these figures appears in your surroundings.

Rectangle	Quadrilateral	Intersecting Lines	Perpendicular Lines
Acute Angle	Obtuse Angle	Right Angle	Trapezoid
Parallelogram	Equilateral Triangle	Isosceles Triangle	Scalene Triangle

Parallel Lines

Rhombus

Circle

©1995 by Incentive Publications, Inc., Nashville, TN.

NAME_____

TANGRAMS

NOTE TO THE TEACHER: Tangrams, one of the most fascinating puzzles available today, can be used effectively in our classrooms to stimulate our students to use logic and also as a tool with which to explore and reinforce basic mathematical concepts. The activities given in this book are only a few ways that tangrams can be used and as you experiment with these activities, you will most likely discover many other ways to use this ancient Chinese puzzle.

These activities can be used by each individual student in large group instruction, cooperative learning teams, or in learning centers.

Below is a Tangram set that can be duplicated and laminated for use with students.

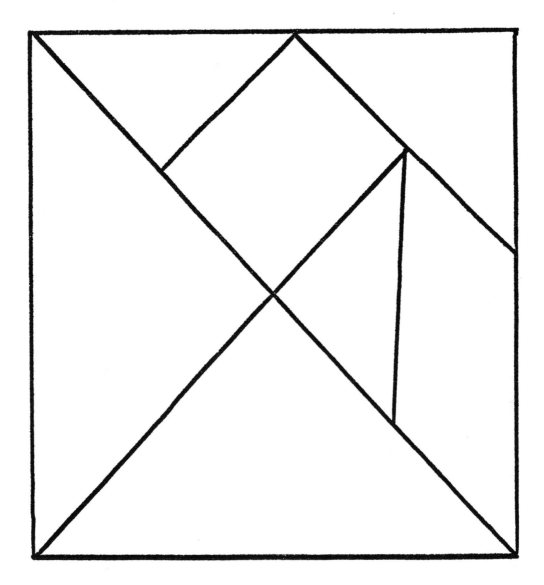

©1995 by Incentive Publications, Inc., Nashville, TN.

NAME_____

TANGRAM MATCH-UP

DIRECTIONS: Cut out the pieces of the puzzle. Then match the geometric term with the geometric figure to solve the puzzle. When you have solved the puzzle, sketch the figure you created on another sheet of paper.

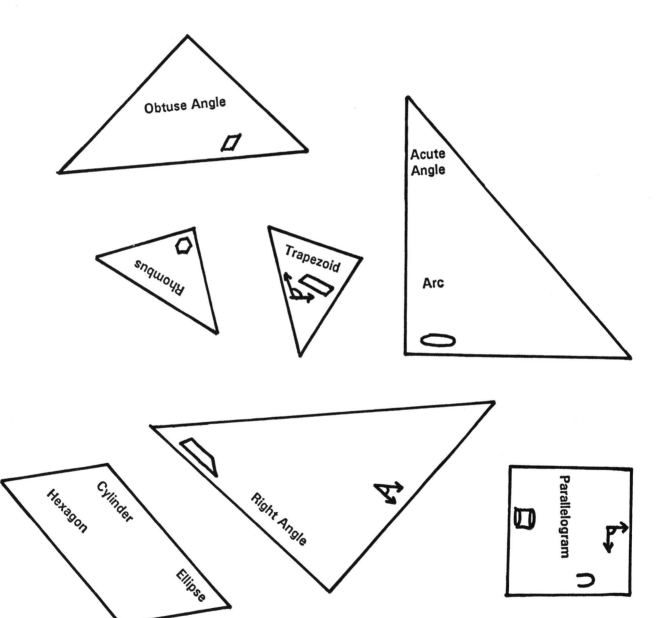

©1995 by Incentive Publications, Inc., Nashville, TN.

NAME_____

Symmetrical Design

DIRECTIONS: Create a design that has 8 or more lines of symmetry. With a ruler, draw in all of your lines of symmetry.

The name of my design is _____

How many lines of symmetry did you put into your design? _____

©1995 by Incentive Publications, Inc., Nashville, TN.

Finding perimeter

What kind of pliers do mathematicians use?

DIRECTIONS: Find the perimeter of each of the figures below. Then, find your answer in the decoder, and each time your answer occurs, write the letter of the problem above it.

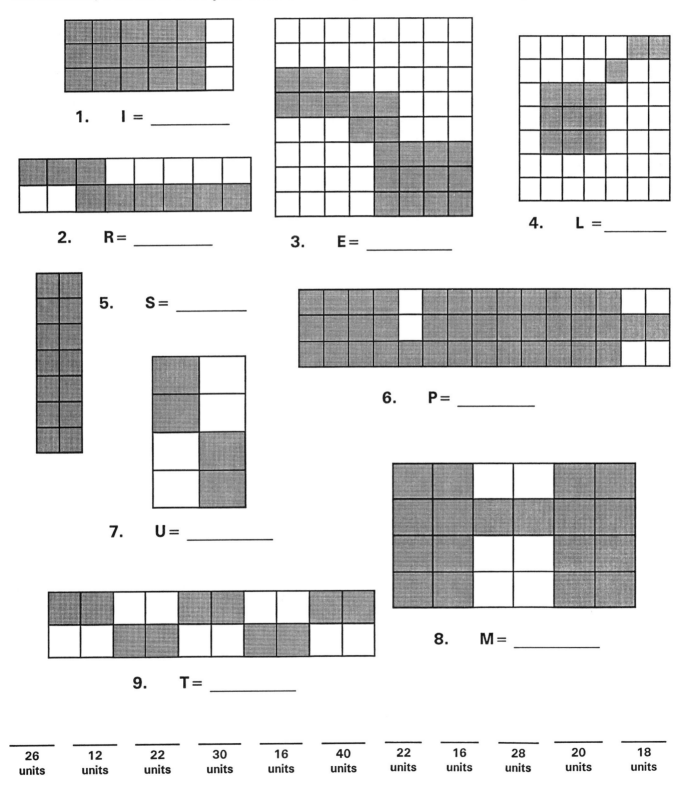

1.   I = _____

2.   R = _____

3.   E = _____

4.   L = _____

5.   S = _____

6.   P = _____

7.   U = _____

8.   M = _____

9.   T = _____

26 units	12 units	22 units	30 units	16 units	40 units	22 units	16 units	28 units	20 units	18 units

©1995 by Incentive Publications, Inc., Nashville, TN.

NAME_____

ANIMALMANIA

BACKGROUND INFORMATION:

(1) I am an insect that spends most of my life sleeping. I sleep for **17** years in the ground, come out for **5** weeks in the sun and then I die.

What am I? _____

(2) My tail is so brittle that if an enemy pulls at it in battle, I will pull my body away and leave my tail behind because I know a new one will grow back in its place.

What am I? _____

DIRECTIONS: To solve the riddles above, find the perimeter of each geometric figure. Then locate your answer in the decoder. Each time your answer appears in the decoder, write the letter of the problem above it.

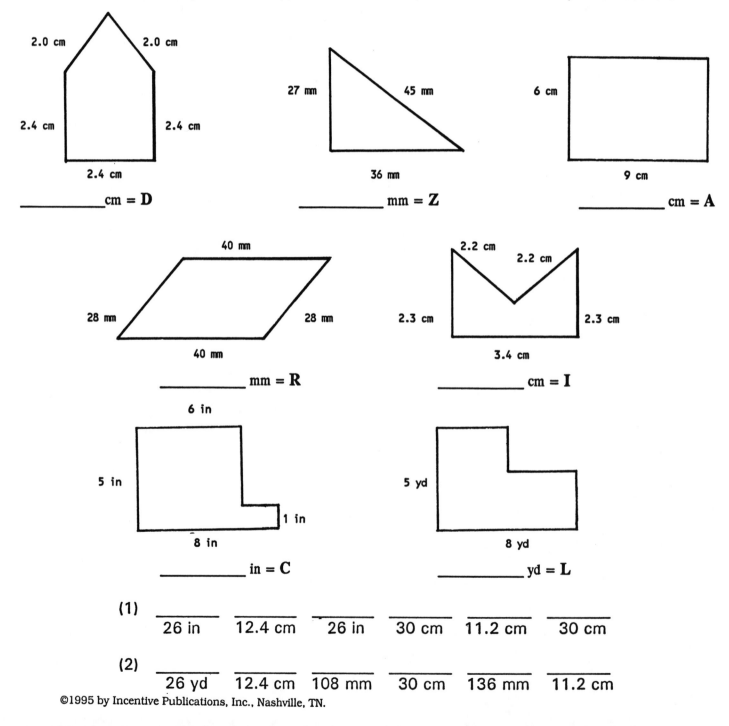

2.0 cm   2.0 cm
2.4 cm   2.4 cm
2.4 cm

_____ cm = **D**

27 mm   45 mm
36 mm

_____ mm = **Z**

6 cm
9 cm

_____ cm = **A**

40 mm
28 mm   28 mm
40 mm

_____ mm = **R**

2.2 cm   2.2 cm
2.3 cm   2.3 cm
3.4 cm

_____ cm = **I**

6 in
5 in
8 in
1 in

_____ in = **C**

5 yd
8 yd

_____ yd = **L**

(1) _____   _____   _____   _____   _____   _____
26 in   12.4 cm   26 in   30 cm   11.2 cm   30 cm

(2) _____   _____   _____   _____   _____   _____
26 yd   12.4 cm   108 mm   30 cm   136 mm   11.2 cm

©1995 by Incentive Publications, Inc., Nashville, TN.

Finding the area of squares and rectangles

What geometric figure is like a runaway parrot?

DIRECTIONS: Find the area of each of the figures below, and then find your answer in the decoder. Each time your answer occurs in the decoder, write the letter of the problem above it.

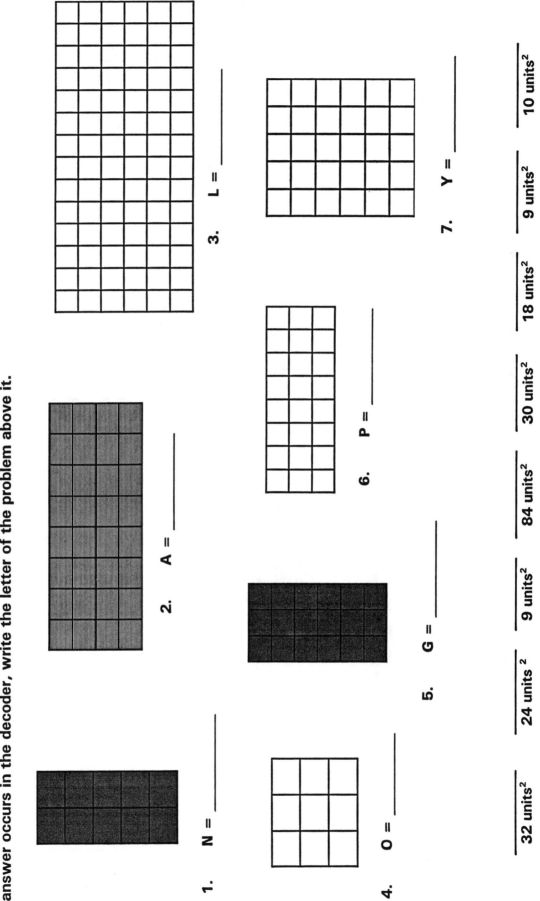

1. N = _____

2. A = _____

3. L = _____

4. O = _____

5. G = _____

6. P = _____

7. Y = _____

32 units²	24 units²	9 units²	84 units²	30 units²	18 units²	9 units²	10 units²

©1995 by Incentive Publications, Inc., Nashville, TN.

Finding the area of rectangles and triangles

How do you know when Cyclopes agree?

DIRECTIONS: Find the area of each rectangle or triangle. Find you answer in the decoder at the bottom of the page. Each time your answer occurs in the decoder, write the letter of the problem above it.

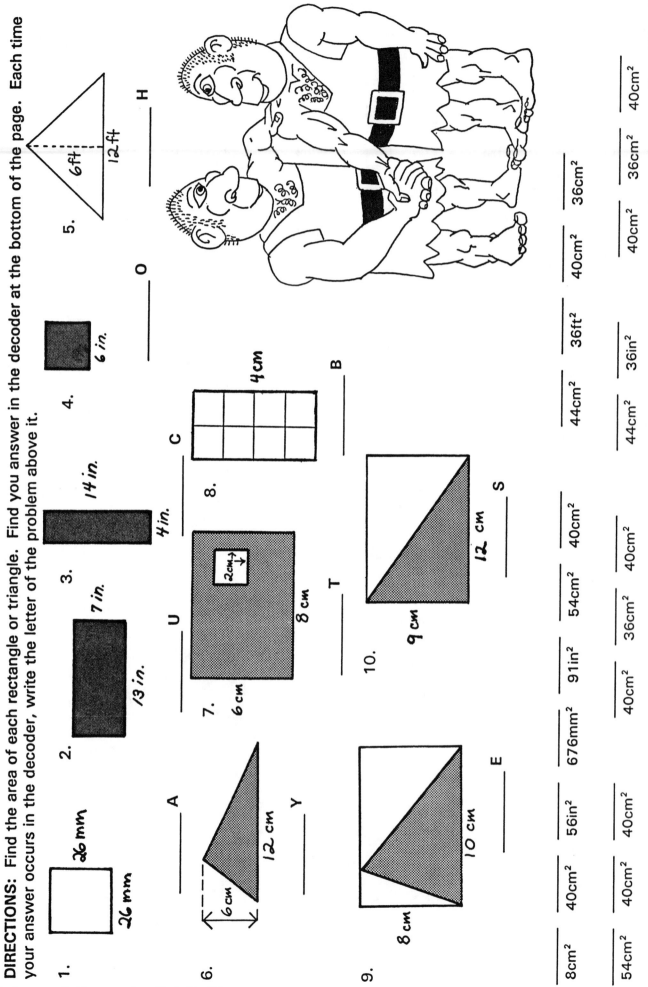

©1995 by Incentive Publications, Inc., Nashville, TN.

Finding the area of polygons

NAME_____

What did Snow White say when her photos were late coming?

DIRECTIONS: Figure out the area of each of the polygons described below. Then find this number in the secret code below. Each time your answer appears in the secret code, write the letter of the problem above it.

Square with side of 30'	sq. ft.	D
Triangle with base of 12' and height of 10'	sq. ft.	R
Rectangle with length of 13' and width of 6'	sq. ft.	A
Parallelogram with base of 50' and height of 20'	sq. ft.	I
Triangle with base of 28' and height of 12'	sq. ft.	L
Rectangle with length of 40' and height of 30'	sq. ft.	O
Triangle with base of 14' and height of 7'	sq. ft.	S
Parallelogram with base of 22' and height of 9'	sq. ft.	Y
Rectangle with width of 82' and length of 100'	sq. ft.	W
Square with side of 4'	sq. ft.	M
Triangle with base of 20' and height of 7'	sq. ft.	P
Rectangle with length of 50' and width of 30'	sq. ft.	N
Square with side of 20'	sq. ft.	C
Parallelogram with base of 100' and height of 35'	sq. ft.	E
Triangle with base of 20' and height of 4'	sq. ft.	T

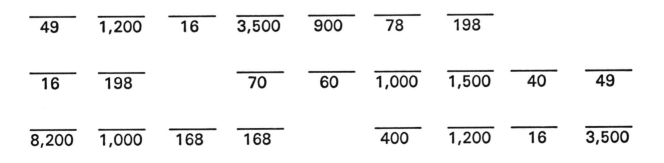

49	1,200	16	3,500	900	78	198		

16	198		70	60	1,000	1,500	40	49

8,200	1,000	168	168		400	1,200	16	3,500

©1995 by Incentive Publications, Inc., Nashville, TN.

Finding the area of circles

©1995 by Incentive Publications, Inc., Nashville, TN.

NAME _____

What did the acorn say when it grew up?

DIRECTIONS: Find the area of each circle below. Find your answer in the secret code at the bottom of the page. Each time your answer appears in the secret code, write the letter of the problem above it.

1. 5"

2. 24"

3. 15"

4. 20"

5. 8"

6. 13"

7. 14"

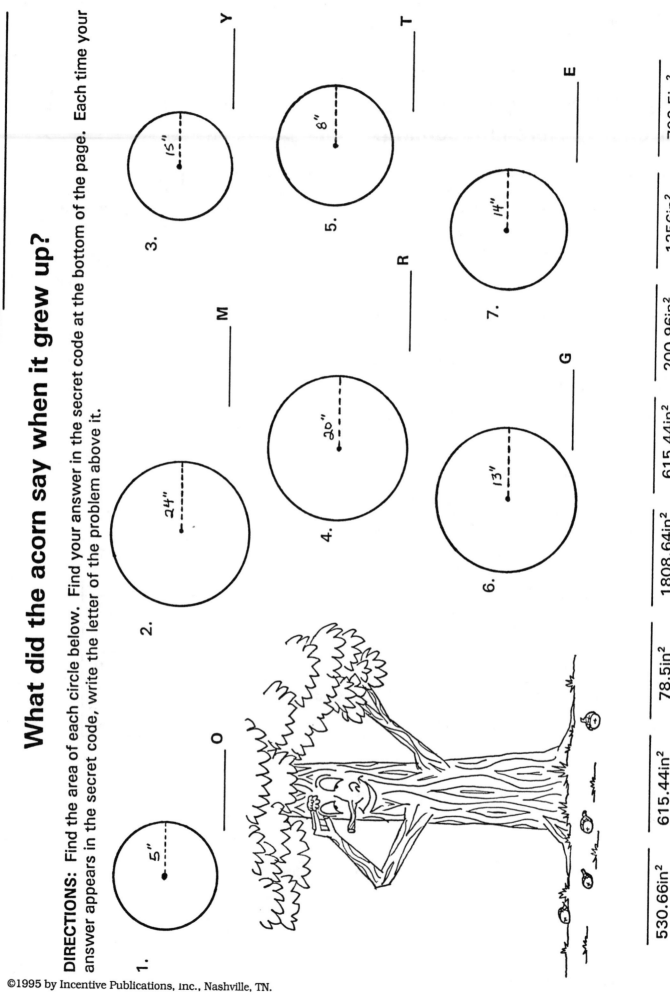

O	M	Y	G	R	T	E

| 530.66in² | 615.44in² | 78.5in² | 1808.64in² | 615.44in² | 200.96in² | 1256in² | 706.5in² |

Finding the volume of rectangular prisms

If all the cars in the world were pink, what would you have?

DIRECTIONS: Figure the volume of the rectangular prisms below and then find your answer in the secret code. Each time your answer appears in the secret code, write the letter of the problem above it.

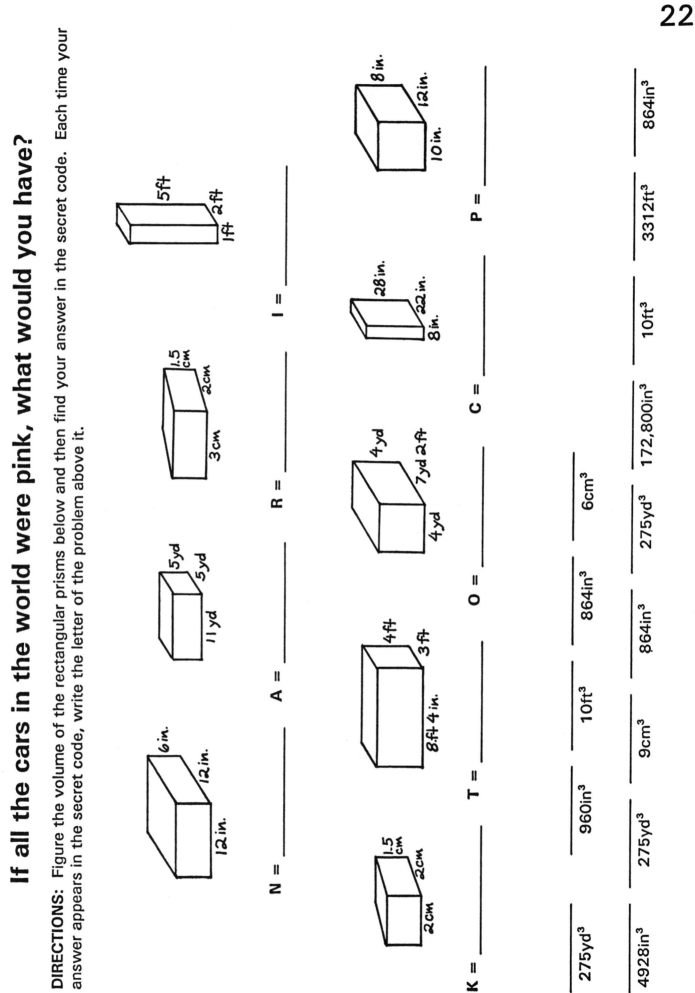

N = _____

A = _____

R = _____

I = _____

K = _____

T = _____

O = _____

C = _____

P = _____

_____	_____	_____	_____	_____	_____
275yd³	960in³	10ft³	864in³	6cm³	

_____	_____	_____	_____	_____	_____
4928in³	275yd³	9cm³	864in³	275yd³	172,800in³	10ft³	3312ft³	864in³

©1995 by Incentive Publications, Inc., Nashville, TN.

NAME

Finding the volume of rectangular prisms

Who invented fractions?

DIRECTIONS: Find the volume of each rectangular prism and then locate the correct answer in the decoder at the bottom of the page. Each time your answer occurs in the decoder, write the letter or fractional number of the problem above it.

1.

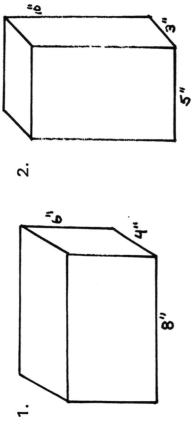

6"
4"
8"

2.

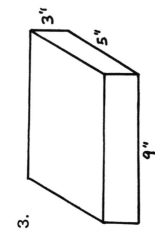

6"
5"
3"

3.

3"
5"
9"

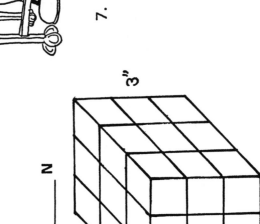

7.

2"
2"
5"

$\frac{1}{8}$

5.

7"
2"
4"
6"
3"
4"

4.

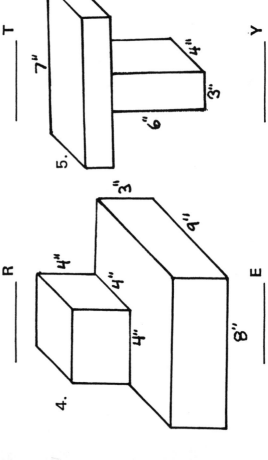

4"
4"
3"
4"
9"
8"

6.

3"
3"
3"

27in³	280in³	135in³	192in³	128in³	150in³	27in³	280in³	20in³
R		T		Y	N		H	
E								

©1995 by Incentive Publications, Inc., Nashville, TN.

Finding volume

NAME _____

Why were Indians the first people in North America?

DIRECTIONS: First, find the volume of the rectangular prisms given below. The length (L), width (W) and height (H) are given. Second, find your answer in the secret code. Each time your answer appears in the secret code write the letter of the problem above it.

V - L = 10 in. W = 5 in. H = 6 in. _____

R - L = 4 cm W = 2 cm H = 1 cm _____

D - L = 4 mm W = 4 mm H = 2 mm _____

O - L = 8 ft. W = 6 ft. H = 10 ft. _____

A - L = 9 yds. W = 3 yds. H = 6 yds. _____

H - L = 2 m W = 1 m H = 5 m _____

Y - L = 6 cm W = 6 cm H = 8 cm _____

S - L = 10 ft. W = 10 ft. H = 10 ft. _____

N - L = 12 in. W = 4 in. H = 5 in. _____

E - L = 7 mm W = 5 mm H = 12 mm _____

T - L = 15 cm W = 10 cm H = $\frac{1}{2}$ cm _____

I - L = 19 cm W = 2 cm H = 10 cm _____

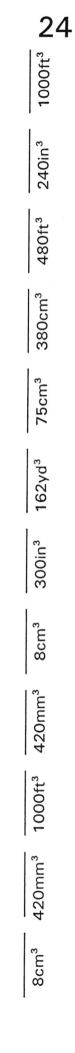

Secret code:

1000ft³ 240in³ 480ft³ 380cm³ 75cm³ 32mm³

162yd³ 162yd³ 10m³ 300in³ 8cm³ 420mm³

1000ft³ 420mm³ 288cm³

75cm³ 10m³ 420mm³ 288cm³

8cm³ 420mm³ 1000ft³ 420mm³

©1995 by Incentive Publications, Inc., Nashville, TN.

NAME_____

What happens when there's an explosion at a hotel?

DIRECTIONS: Solve each problem below and then find your answer in the decoder at the bottom of the page. Each time your answer occurs in the decoder, write the letter of the problem above it.

Find the perimeter - Add the measurements of each of the sides.

1. Square - Each side measures 16 ft. _____ **N**
2. Rectangle - One side measures 4 ft. and the other measures 6 ft. _____ **L**
3. Triangle - One side measures 10 in., another side measures 12 in. and the third side measures 8 in. _____ **R**

Find the area - Multiply to find the area of the rectangle, square or triangle.

4. L = 7 m, W = 8 m _____ **I**
5. L = 15 cm, W = 15 cm _____ **S**
6. a square - one side is 42 yards _____ **M**
7. a triangle - base is 8 ft. and height is 5 ft. _____ **G**
8. a triangle - base is 30 m and height is 10 m _____ **A**

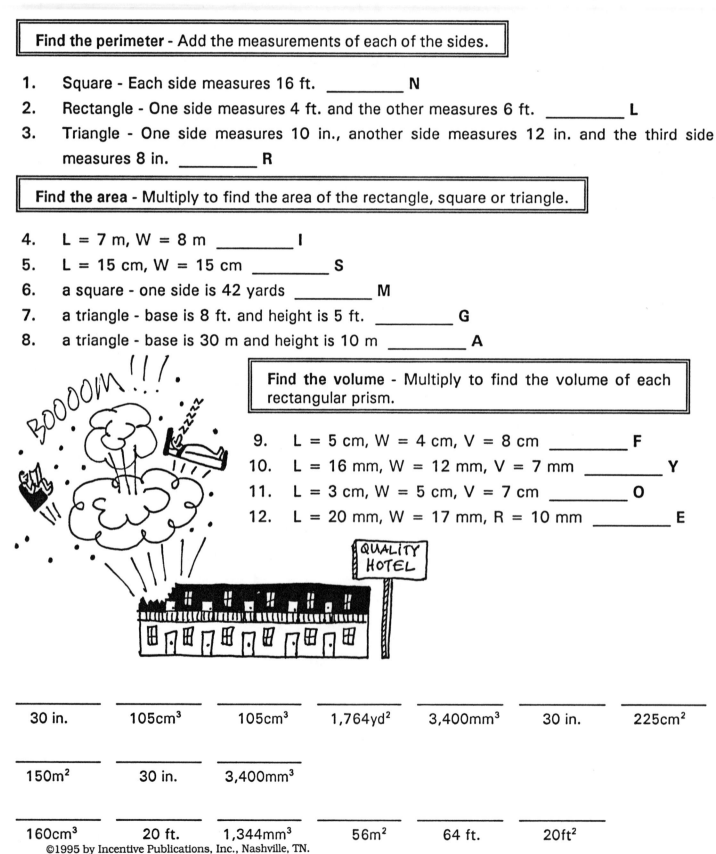

Find the volume - Multiply to find the volume of each rectangular prism.

9. L = 5 cm, W = 4 cm, V = 8 cm _____ **F**
10. L = 16 mm, W = 12 mm, V = 7 mm _____ **Y**
11. L = 3 cm, W = 5 cm, V = 7 cm _____ **O**
12. L = 20 mm, W = 17 mm, R = 10 mm _____ **E**

---

30 in.	105cm³	105cm³	1,764yd²	3,400mm³	30 in.	225cm²

150m²	30 in.	3,400mm³

160cm³	20 ft.	1,344mm³	56m²	64 ft.	20ft²

©1995 by Incentive Publications, Inc., Nashville, TN.

Solving geometric problems involving perimeter, area, and volume

NAME_____

What time is it when you have a toothache?

DIRECTIONS: Solve each problem below and then find your answer in the decoder at the bottom of the page. Each time you answer occurs in the decoder, write the letter of the problem above it.

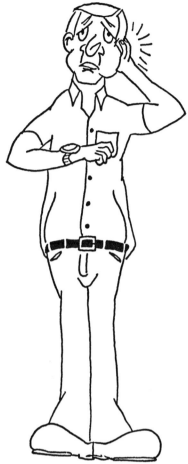

1. Chad has a toolbox that is 2 feet in length, 1 foot wide, and 1 foot in height. What is the volume of Chad's toolbox? _____ **U**

2. Gray is planning to recarpet her room. The length of her room is 20 feet and the width is 12 feet. How much carpet does Gray need for her room? _____ **Y**

3. Apollo 8, one of the missions to the Moon, planned to land its capsule in an area of the Atlantic Ocean. If the section of the water the astronauts planned to splash down in was 13 miles long by 11 miles wide, what was the splashdown area in square miles? _____ **R**

4. Adrienne is planning to run in a race on July 4th. In preparation for this race she runs around a large auditorium 8 times without stopping. If the four sides of the auditorium are each 110 feet, how many total feet did she run each day? _____ **I**

5. Ben has bought a new aquarium that is 22 in. long, 9 in. wide, and 8 in. high. How much water can Ben put in his aquarium if he fills it up to the top? _____ **S**

6. Ernie is going to line off the perimeter of the football field for his next game. The length of the field is 120 yards and the width is 160 feet. How many total feet will Ernie be chalking in order to have the entire field lined? _____ **O**

7. If Brooke's bathtub is 4 ft. long, 2 ft. wide, and 2 ft. high, how much water will Brooke use if she fills her tub one-half full? _____ **H**

8. Johnny and Zack have planned for their treehouse to be 4 ft. long and 3 ft. wide. How much lumber do they need to buy for their floor? _____ **T**

_____	_____	_____
3,520ft.	12ft²	1,584in³

_____	_____	_____	_____	_____	__
12ft²	1,040ft.	1,040ft.	12ft²	8ft³	

_____	_____	_____	_____	_____
8ft³	2ft³	143mi²	12ft²	240ft²

©1995 by Incentive Publications, Inc., Nashville, TN.

NAME_____

Constructing Solid Figures—A Cube

DIRECTIONS: Cut along the dark heavy lines... ✄
Fold on the lines that are dashes... ✂
Tape or glue tabs... ✍

After you have constructed your cube, complete the section on the cube on the "Data Sheet - Part I".

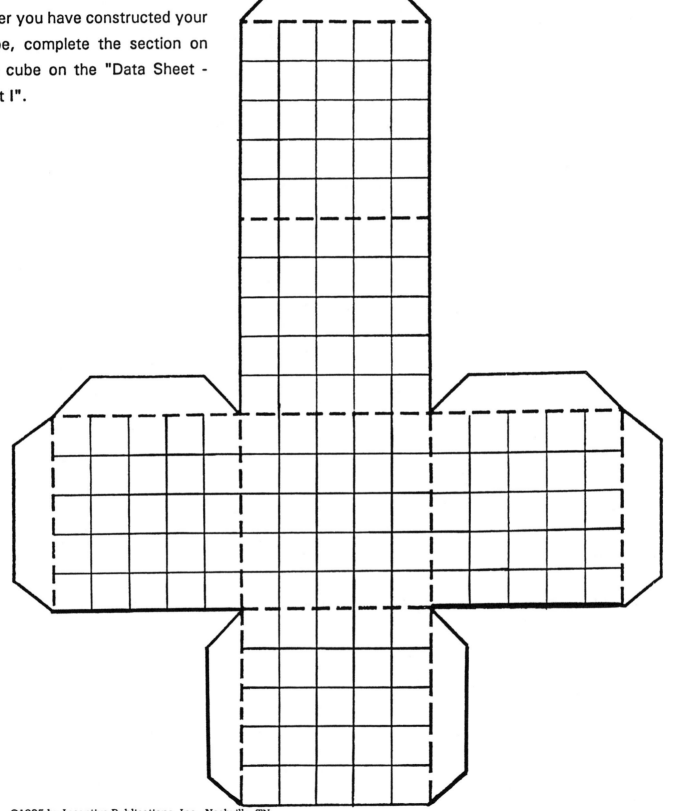

©1995 by Incentive Publications, Inc., Nashville, TN.

NAME_____

Constructing Solid Figures—A Rectangular Prism

DIRECTIONS: Cut along the dark heavy lines... ✂

Fold on the lines that are dashes... ✎

Tape or glue tabs... ✐

After you have constructed your rectangular prism, complete the section on the rectangular prism on the "Data Sheet - Part I".

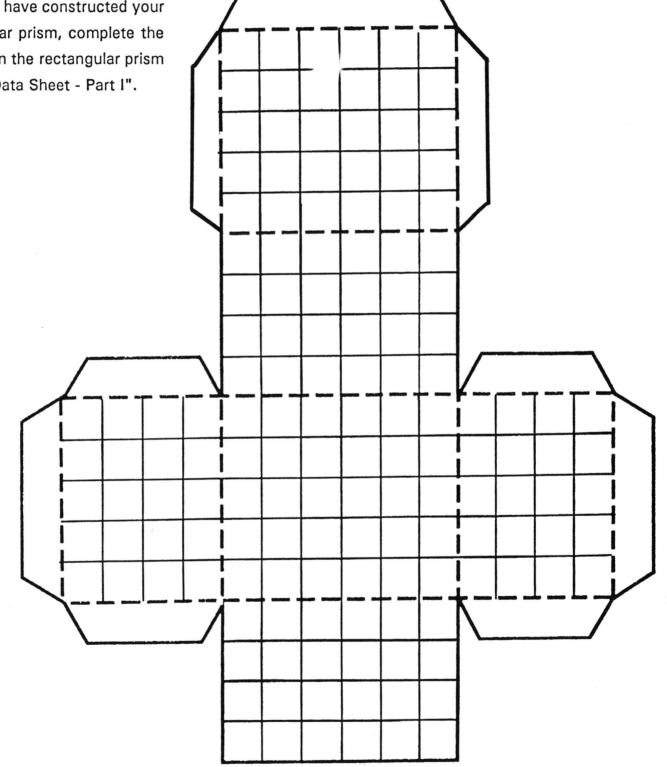

©1995 by Incentive Publications, Inc., Nashville, TN.

NAME_____

DATA SHEET - Part 1
A CUBE AND A RECTANGULAR PRISM

DIRECTIONS: Give the information requested below after constructing each figure. *Use with pages 27-28.*

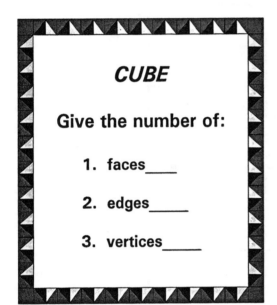

CUBE

Give the number of:

1. faces____

2. edges_____

3. vertices_____

Find the volume of the cube in cubic units by using the formula, $V = L \times W \times H$.

4. The volume of the cube is _____ cubic units.

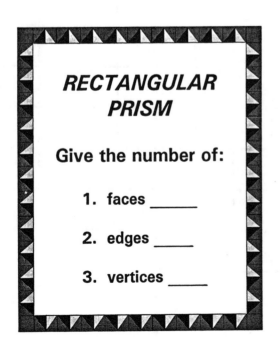

RECTANGULAR PRISM

Give the number of:

1. faces _____

2. edges _____

3. vertices _____

Find the volume of the rectangular prism.

4. The volume is _____ cubic units.

©1995 by Incentive Publications, Inc., Nashville, TN.

NAME _____

Constructing Solid Figures— A Square Pyramid

Constructing a pyramid

DIRECTIONS: Cut along the dark heavy lines... ✂️

Fold on the lines that are dashes... 📄

Tape or glue tabs... 📐.

After you have constructed your pyramid, complete the section on the pyramid on the "Data Sheet-Part II".

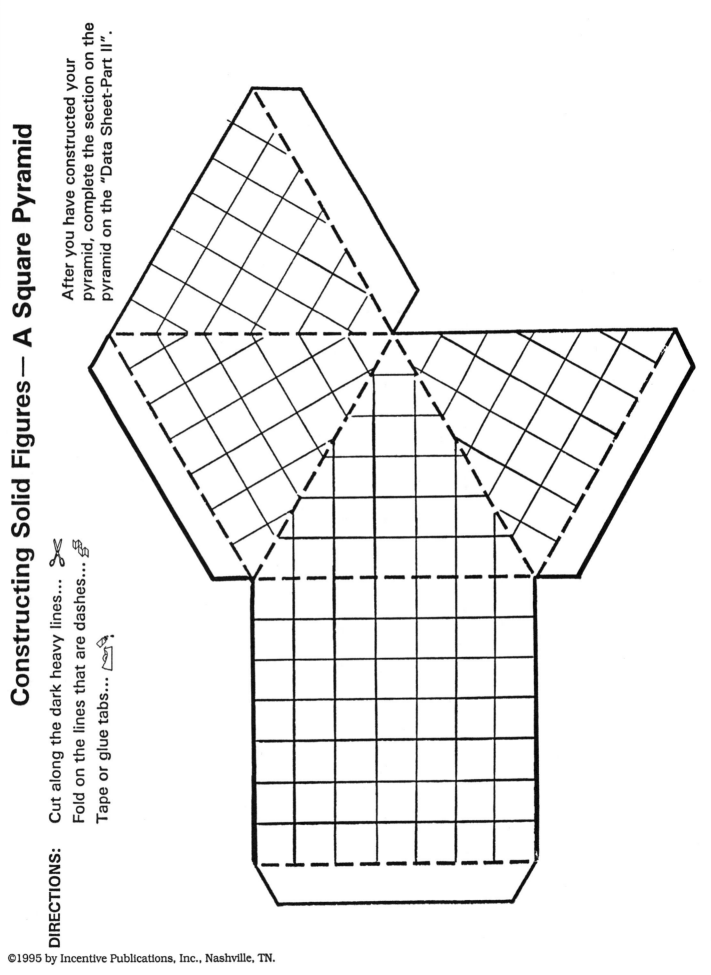

©1995 by Incentive Publications, Inc., Nashville, TN.

Constructing a cylinder

Constructing Solid Figures—A Cylinder

After you have constructed your cylinder, complete the section on the cylinder on the "Data Sheet-Part II".

DIRECTIONS: Cut along the dark heavy lines… ✂

Fold on the lines that are dashes… 🏳

Tape or glue tabs… 🖌

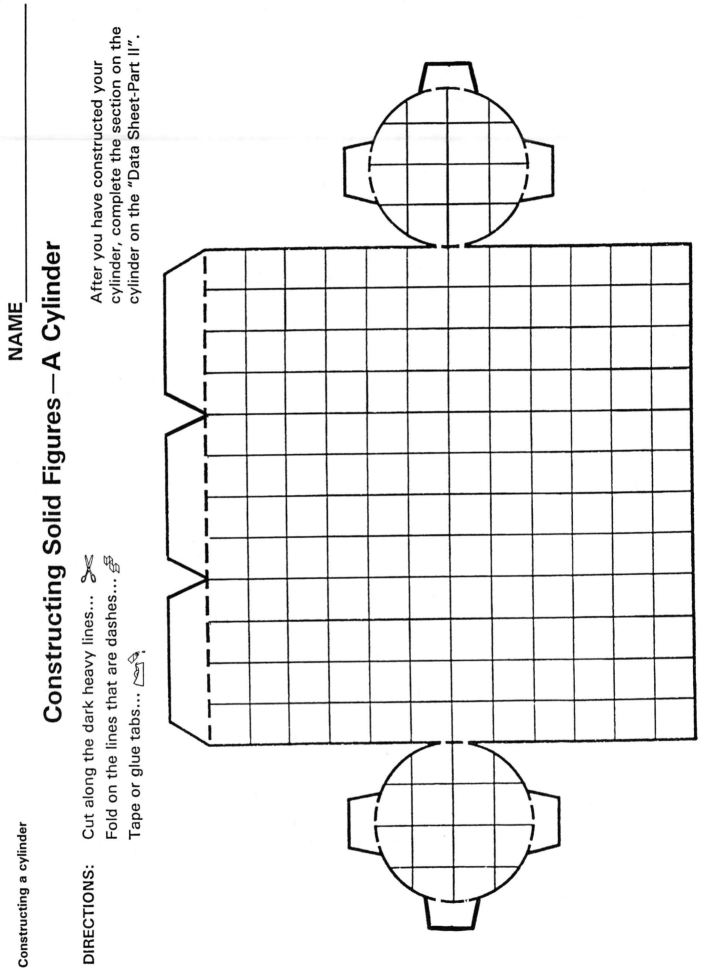

©1995 by Incentive Publications, Inc., Nashville, TN.

NAME_____

DATA SHEET - Part 2
A SQUARE PYRAMID AND A CYLINDER

DIRECTIONS: Give the information requested below after constructing each figure. *(Use with pages 30-31).*

SQUARE PYRAMID

Give the number of:

1. faces_____

2. edges_____

3. vertices_____

CYLINDER

Give the number of:

1. faces_____

2. edges_____

3. vertices_____

Extension: Create a teaching aid for another solid figure such as a triangular prism, sphere, etc. Ask a friend to follow your directions and see if he/she can construct your figure.

©1995 by Incentive Publications, Inc., Nashville, TN.

Finding examples of solid figures

SOLID FIGURES

NAME

DIRECTIONS: Investigate your environment and find and draw objects that are examples of the solid figures listed below.

An example of a cylinder would be [COLA can image] or [triangular prism image] a triangular prism.

Cone	Cube	Triangular prism	Rectangular prism
Hexagonal prism	Pentagonal prism	Triangular pyramid	Square pyramid
Rectangular pyramid	Hexagonal pyramid	Cylinder	Sphere

©1995 by Incentive Publications, Inc., Nashville, TN.

NAME_____

Specialized Spelling List - Geometry

DIRECTIONS: Draw a picture of each term and label it. Learn to spell each of these and be able to draw a diagram of each.

1.	line	26.	sphere
2.	ray	27.	cube
3.	line segment	28.	cone
4.	angle	29.	cylinder
5.	right angle	30.	rectangular prism
6.	obtuse angle	31.	triangular prism
7.	acute angle	32.	square pyramid
8.	polygon	33.	volume (formula)
9.	quadrilateral	34.	area of a rectangle (formula)
10.	square	35.	area of a triangle (formula)
11.	rectangle	36.	perimeter
12.	triangle	37.	congruent
13.	equilateral triangle	38.	symmetry
14.	isosceles triangle	39.	circumference
15.	scalene triangle	40.	diameter
16.	right triangle	41.	radius
17.	trapezoid	42.	chord
18.	rhombus	43.	protractor
19.	parallelogram	44.	compass
20.	pentagon	45.	vertex
21.	hexagon	46.	straight angle
22.	octagon	47.	hexagonal prism
23.	parallel lines	48.	triangular pyramid
24.	perpendicular lines	49.	faces
25.	intersecting lines	50.	geometry

©1995 by Incentive Publications, Inc., Nashville, TN.

NAME_____

An ABC Book of Geometry

DIRECTIONS: Put together a booklet with a cover and 27 pages. Design your cover and include the title, *An ABC Book of Geometric Terms.* The first page will be your title page and should include such information as the name of your booklet, your name, the publisher, and the date. (See example 1). On the second page, write the letter *A,* and then think of the many, varied and unusual words beginning with the letter A that are associated with geometry. Choose one of the words you thought of and write it, create a drawing to show you understand the meaning of the word and, finally, write a definition for the word. (See example 2). Complete the other 25 pages in the same manner.

It's important to use a straightedge for your drawings. You may want to add color to give your book a more professional look.

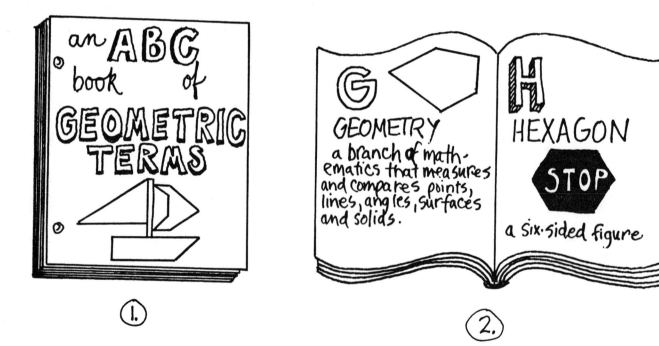

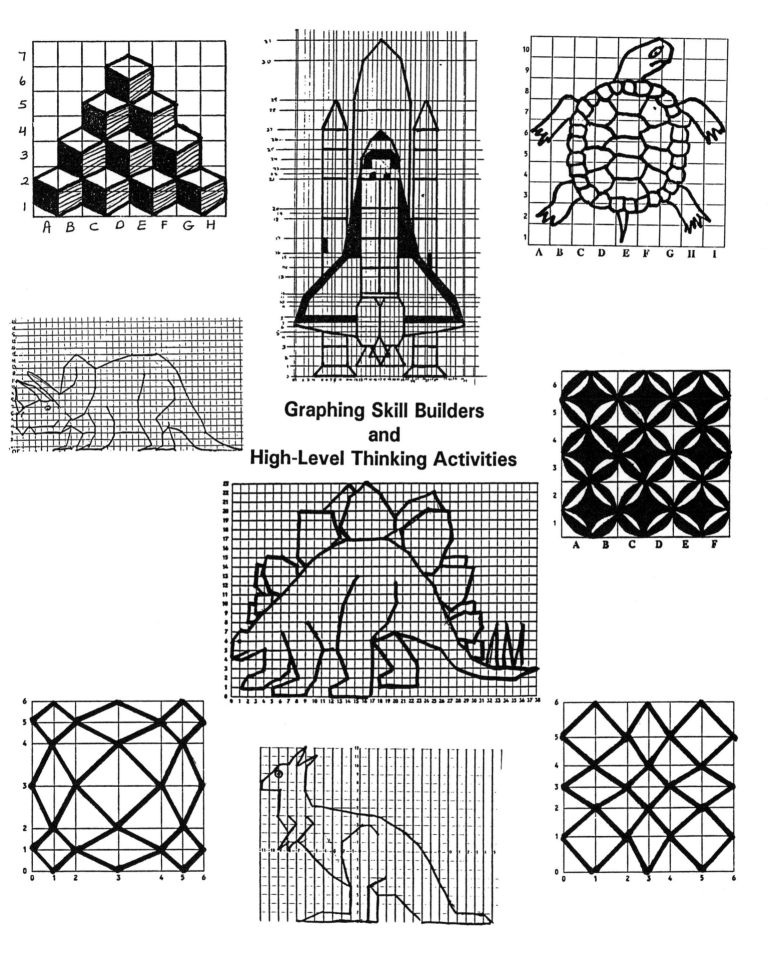

Graphing Skill Builders
and
High-Level Thinking Activities

©1995 by Incentive Publications, Inc., Nashville, TN.

NAME_____

Why is this a star for an eleven year old?

DIRECTIONS: The star is made of one continuous line. Use a ruler to draw and connect your lines.

(10,24), (18,1), (4,21), (23,5), (0,15), (25,12), (1,8), (23,19), (5,2), (17,24), (11,0), (10,24).

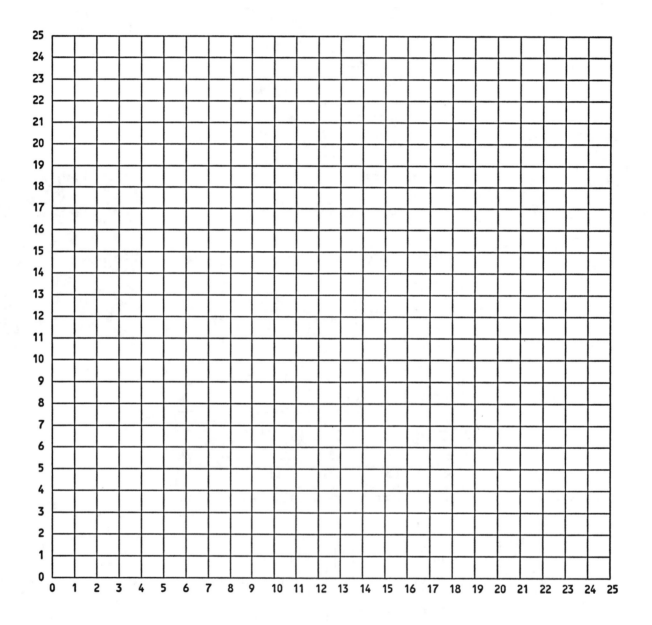

Answer to riddle: _____

_____

©1995 by Incentive Publications, Inc., Nashville, TN.

NAME_____

What bird prefers subfreezing temperatures and cannot fly?

BACKGROUND INFORMATION: I am most comfortable in subfreezing temperatures. In fact, the San Diego Zoo made a special subfreezing habitat for my species. Even though we can't fly, we are incredible divers and can stay under water for 18 minutes. The largest of us is called "Emperor" and we can grow to a height of 4 feet.

What am I? _____

DIRECTIONS: This graph is made up of several lines. The symbol [denotes the beginning of a line, and the symbol] denotes the end of a line. Graph the coordinates in the order given below.

[(3,12), (1,13), (3,14), (4,15), (5,15), (6,14), (6,12), (8,9), (9,3), (10,1), (9,1)].

[(9,2), (9,0), (5,0), (7,1), (5,1), (3,4), (2,6), (2,10), (3,12), (5,12), (6,10), (4,7), (4,6), (5,4), (7,2), (6,6), (7,8)].

[(1,13), (3,13)].

[(2,10), (1,8), (0,5), (0,2), (1,5), (2,6)].

[(5,1), (3,0), (5,0)].

Next draw an eye, like this ⊙, around the point (4,14).

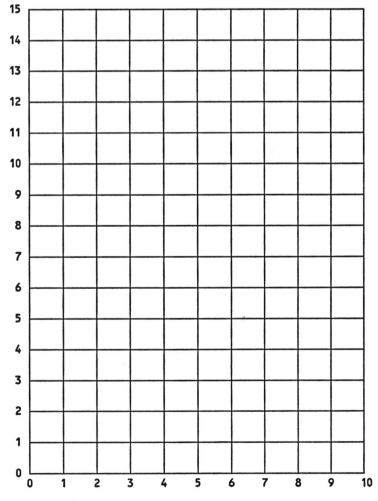

©1995 by Incentive Publications, Inc., Nashville, TN.

Graphing coordinates

Transforming a Triangle into a Chocolate Kiss

DIRECTIONS: We will accomplish this by using an uneven grid. Graph the coordinates in the order given on each grid. These coordinates will produce one closed line.

(0,0), (1,1), (2,2), (3,3), (4,4), (5,5), (6,4), (7,3), (8,2), (9,1), (10,0), (0,0)

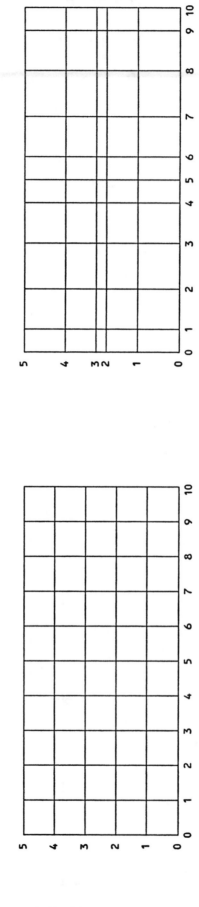

©1995 by Incentive Publications, Inc., Nashville, TN.

Graphing coordinates

NAME_____

What animal is the most powerful
winged predator of the night?

BACKGROUND INFORMATION: I feed mostly on mice but I am capable of taking on a skunk. Since I cannot look to each side, I can turn my head farther around than most of my other soft feathered friends.

What am I? _____

DIRECTIONS: This graph is made up of several lines. The symbol [denotes the beginning of a line, and the symbol] denotes the end of a line. Graph the coordinates in the order given below.

[(0,2), (12,2), (12,3), (13,3), (12,2), (16,2), (16,3), (15,3), (16,2), (21,2), (22,3), (16,3), (23,15), (18,23), (10, 23), (6,15), (12,3), (0,3)]. [(13,2), (14,0), (15,2)]. [(7,17), (6,17), (4,15), (0,5), (9,9)]. [(19,9), (28,5), (25,15), (23,17), (22,17)]. [(6,15), (14,18), (22,15)]. [(10,23), (12,21), (16,21), (18,23)]. [(13,21), (14,19), (15,21)].

Next draw a pair of eyes, like this ☉, around the the points (12,20) and ·(16,20).

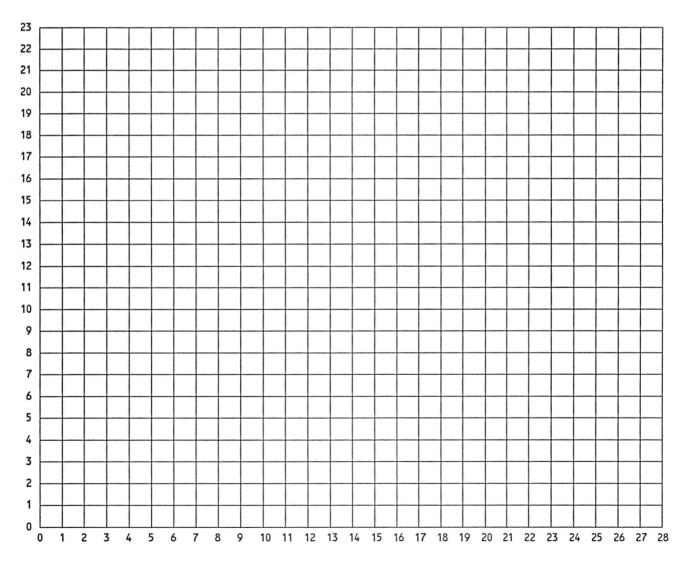

©1995 by Incentive Publications, Inc., Nashville, TN.

Graphing coordinates

Which present-day fish lived on earth during the time of the dinosaurs?

BACKGROUND INFORMATION: I've been around since before the dinosaurs. I have changed little over the years; that's because I am an efficient predator. Some of my species are the largest fish in the ocean.

What am I?

DIRECTIONS: This graph is made up of several lines. The symbol [denotes the beginning of a line, and the symbol] denotes the end of a line. Graph the coordinates in the order given below.

[(0,7), (2,8), (5,9), (10,10), (19,10), (25,9), (28,8), (32,8), (37,14), (39,16), (36,7), (38,2), (32,6), (28,5), (26,5), (20,4), (15,4), (11,5), (11,4), (9,4), (5,5), (3,6), (0,7)]. [(14,10), (15,12), (17,13), (21,14), (19,10)]. [(25,9), (29,10), (28,8)]. [(20,4), (21,3), (18,3), (17,4)]. [(15,4), (16,2), (18,0), (15,0), (13,1), (12,2), (11,4)]. [(3,6), (6,6)]. [(7,6), (7,7), (8,8)]. [(8,6), (8,7), (9,8)]. [(9,6), (9,7), (10,8)]. [(10,6), (10,7), (11,8)]. [(11,6), (11,7), (12,8)].

©1995 by Incentive Publications, Inc., Nashville, TN.

Graphing coordinates

Design Distortion

DIRECTIONS: You can distort a design by using uneven grids. The set of coordinates given below make one continuous line. Graph the coordinates in the order given on each grid to get three different designs.

(1,4), (2,3), (1,2), (0,3), (2,1), (3,0), (4,1), (5,2), (6,3), (5,4), (4,5), (3,6), (2,5), (1,4), (0,5), (1,6),

(2,5), (3,4), (4,5), (5,6), (6,5), (5,4), (4,3), (5,2), (6,1), (5,0), (4,1), (3,2), (2,1), (1,0), (0,1), (1,2),

(2,3), (3,2), (4,3), (3,4), (2,3), (1,4), (0,3)

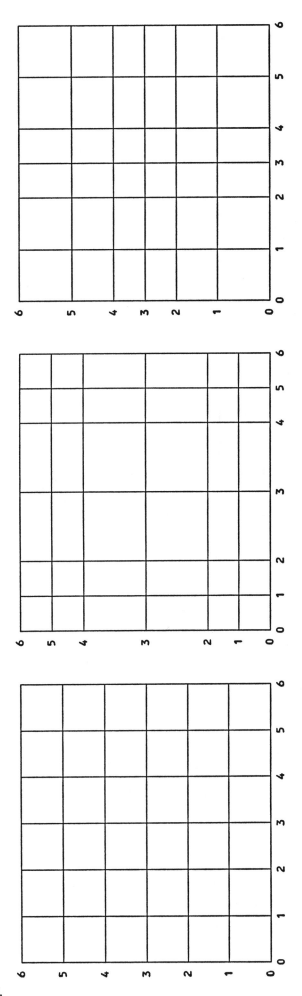

©1995 by Incentive Publications, Inc., Nashville, TN.

NAME_____

What flower is one of the first signs of spring?

What am I? _____

DIRECTIONS: This graph is made up of several lines. The symbol [denotes the beginning of a line, and the symbol] denotes the end of a line. Graph the coordinates in the order given below.

[(6,11), (4,9), (3,7), (2,4), (1,0), (2,0) (4,6) (6,9)]. [(12,17), (10,18), (6,18), (2,17), (0,15), (1,13), (3,12), (6,11), (7,11), (9,12), (12,14)]. [(13,13), (14,9), (15,7), (17,5), (19,4), (22,4) (22,9), (21,12), (19,14)]. [(19,19), (20,20), (21,22), (21,26), (20,29), (18,28), (17,27), (14,23), (13,21), (13,18)]. [(7,11), (6,9), (6,7), (7,4), (11,6), (14,9)]. [(20,13), (24,14), (26,15), (27,17), (24,19), (20,20)]. [(14,23), (12,25), (10,26), (7,27), (6,23), (7,20), (8,18)]. [(15,19), (13,18), (12,17), (12,14), (13,13), (18,13), (19,14), (20,16), (20,17), (19,19), (17,20), (15,19), (14,17), (14,16), (15,14), (16,13)].

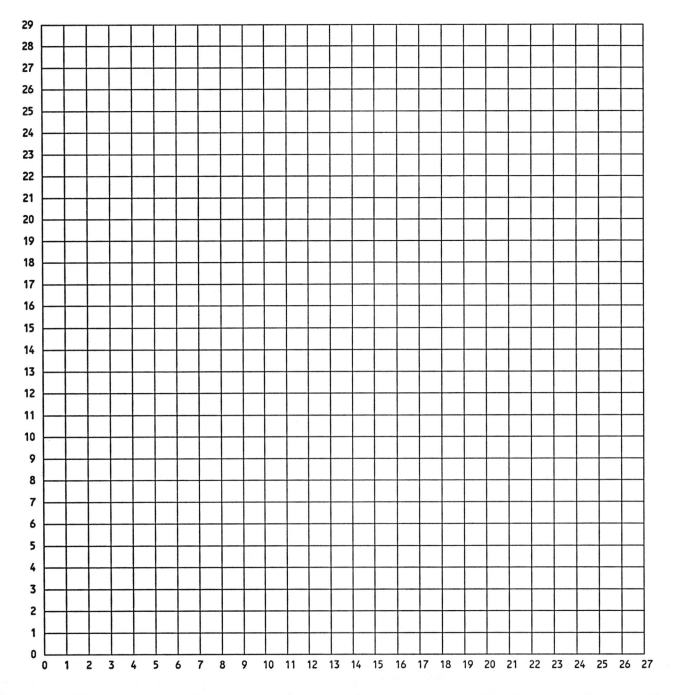

©1995 by Incentive Publications, Inc., Nashville, TN.

Graphing coordinates   NAME_____

What weapon is used for defense on a gunboat?

DIRECTIONS: This graph is made up of several lines. The symbol [denotes the beginning of a line, and the symbol] denotes the end of a line. Graph the coordinates in the order given below.

[(19,0), (2,0), (5,3), (5,5), (6,5), (6,6), (7,6), (7,8), (8,8), (7,9), (7,10), (6,9), (2,13), (3,14), (7,11), (8,13), (9,12), (8,11), (8,9), (9,8), (10,9), (11,9), (11,11), (9,13), (10,14), (8,16), (9,17), (8,19), (6,19), (5,18)]. [(9,17), (15,23), (16,22), (19,25), (22,22), (19,19), (20,18), (13,11), (12,11), (12,9), (13,9) (14,8), (14,3), (15,3), (19,0)]. [(8,8), (8,3), (14,3), (5,3)]. [(19,24), (25,30), (27,28), (21,22)]. [(25,29), (30,34), (31,33), (26,28)].
Shade in your drawing.

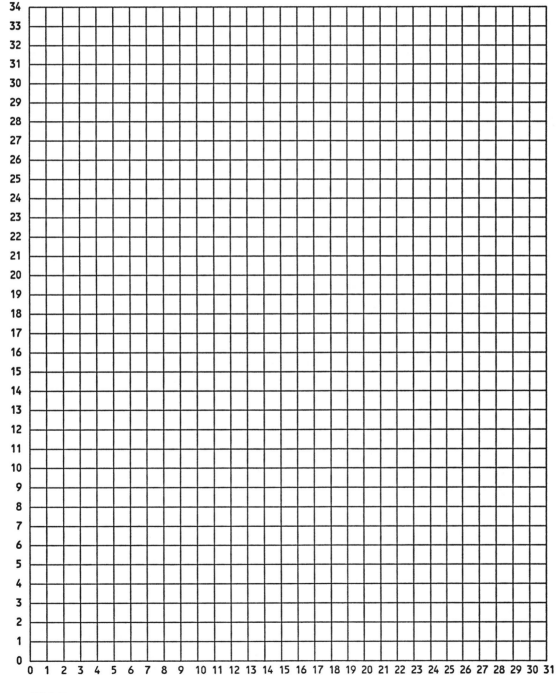

Answer to Riddle: _____

45

NAME _____

What kind of dinosaur had three horns and was carnivorous?

BACKGROUND INFORMATION: I belonged to the last group of dinosaurs to appear on earth. I looked much like our present-day rhinoceroses, but I was much larger. I had a big fringe growing from the back of my skull to protect my neck.

What kind of dinosaur was I? _____

DIRECTIONS: This graph is made up of several lines. The symbol [denotes the beginning of a line, and the symbol] denotes the end of a line. Graph the coordinates in the order given below.

[(8,7), (7,8), (5,8), (2,7), (1,6), (1,4), (2,3), (3,4), (7,4), (8,5)]. [(3,4), (4,3), (8,3), (10,5)]. [(9,6), (10,5), (12,6), (14,10), (14,13), (13,14), (11,15), (9,13), (8,9)]. [(11,13), (10,10), (8,9), (5,11), (2,12), (5,10), (7,8), (4,10), (1,11), (4,9), (5,8)]. [(2,7), (1,8), (0,10), (0,8), (1,6)]. [(14,13), (20,15), (24,15), (26,14), (27,13), (32,3), (35,1), (38,0), (32,0), (30,1), (28,3), (26,4), (25,3)]. [(9,4), (10,4), (12,3), (14,3)]. [(17,3), (22,3)]. [(10,4), (9,1), (7,0), (10,0), (11,1), (12,3)]. [(13,6), (14,4), (14,3), (13,1), (11,0), (15,0), (16,1), (17,3), (17,5), (16,7)]. [(22,12), (21,8), (21,5), (23,1), (21,0), (24,0), (25,1), (25,3), (24,5), (27,8), (27,10), (26,11)]. [(24,0), (27,0), (27,1), (26,4)].

Now draw an eye, like this ⊙, around the point (6,7), and draw a nose, like this ⊂, around the point (2,6).

©1995 by Incentive Publications, Inc., Nashville, TN.

Graphing coordinates   NAME_____

What animal has 40,000 muscles in its nose?

BACKGROUND INFORMATION: I am the largest mammal on land. With my nose I can pull a tree out of the ground, untie a knot, or pick up a string from the floor. Unfortunately, because of my ivory tusks, I have become an endangered species.

What am I? _____

DIRECTIONS: This graph is made up of several lines. The symbol [denotes the beginning of a line, and the symbol] denotes the end of a line. Graph the coordinates in the order given below.

[(3,15), (2,16), (3,18), (4,21), (5,20), (6,21), (8,21), (9,20), (12,19), (14,18), (14,17), (12,14), (10,12), (9,13), (9,18)]. [(9,20), (11,20), (16,19), (19,18), (23,16), (25,13), (25,4), (24,8)]. [(25,11), (24,8), (24,0), (21,0), (22,2), (21,6), (20,8)]. [(22,11), (21,9), (20,8), (18,7), (15,7)]. [(18,7), (19,2), (18,0), (21,0), (21,6)]. [(16,12), (16,10), (15,7), (15,0), (12,0), (13,2), (12,7), (11,11)]. [(9,12), (10,9), (12,7)]. [(8,12), (9,9), (9,2), (8,0), (11,0), (12,7)]. [(4,17), (3,15), (2,11), (2,10), (1,7), (2,3), (3,1), (5,1), (5,2), (4,2), (3,4), (3,8), (4,10)]. [(2,11), (0,9), (2,10)]. [(6,13), (2,9), (4,10), (6,12)]. [(7,14), (6,12), (6,11), (8,12), (9,13)].

Now draw an eye like this ● around the point (6,16).

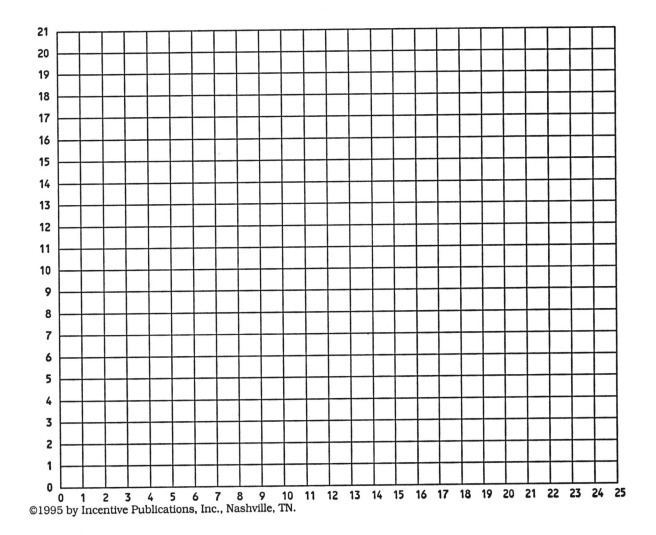

©1995 by Incentive Publications, Inc., Nashville, TN.

NAME

Graphing coordinates

UNITED STATES MAP

DIRECTIONS: Draw a map of the United States in one continuous line by using the coordinates given below: (Use a ruler to connect your points.)

(2,27), (2,25), (1,20), (0,18), (2,11), (5,8), (7,8), (10,6), (14,6), (17,3), (18,4), (19,4), (22,0), (23,0), (23,2), (25,4), (31,4), (30,5), (31,6), (35,6), (36,5), (38,1), (39,1), (39,3), (37,7), (37,9), (40,12), (40,14), (40,15), (41,18), (41,20), (42,21), (43,21), (43,22), (42,21), (42,23), (43,25), (44,26), (42,28), (41,28), (41,25), (39,24), (38,22), (36,21), (35,19), (33,18), (33,21), (32,21), (31,22), (30,18), (29,18), (29,21), (31,23), (29,23), (29,24), (27,23), (26,23), (27,24), (23,25), (19,25), (9,26), (4,27), (4,26), (3,27), (2,27).

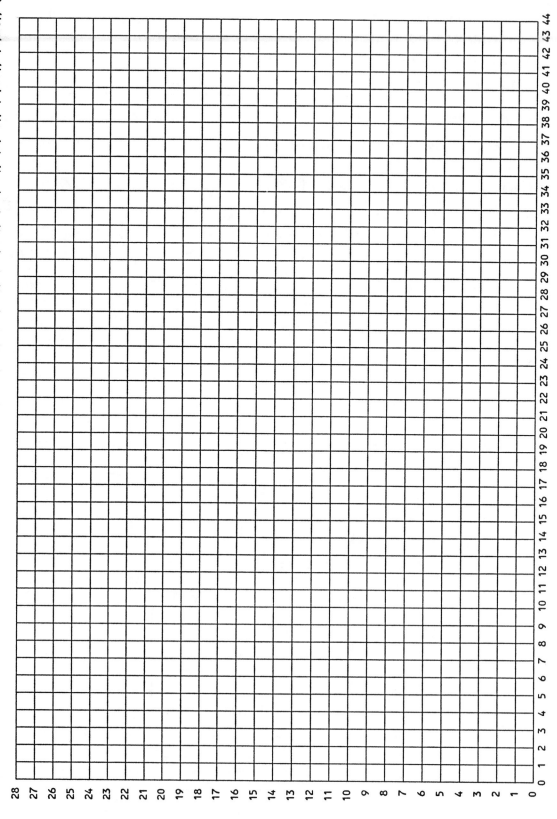

©1995 by Incentive Publications, Inc., Nashville, TN.

Graphing coordinates   NAME_____

What dinosaur used spikes to help it fight its enemies?

BACKGROUND INFORMATION: I was a dinosaur with plates along my back and spikes on my tail. My plates helped keep me cool, and the spikes helped me fight my enemies.

What was I? _____

DIRECTIONS: This graph is made up of several lines. The symbol [denotes the beginning of a line and the symbol] denotes the end of a line. Connect the coordinates in the order given below.

[(2,7), (3,8), (4,9), (5,10), (6,11), (8,13), (9,14), (10,15), (12,16), (14,17), (19,17), (21,16), (24,13), (25,12), (26,10), (27,8), (28,6), (29,5), (30,4), (32,3), (38,3), (35,2), (32,2), (28,3), (25,5), (23,6), (20,7), (17,6)]. [(3,7), (1,7), (0,6), (0,4), (1,4), (4,5), (7,5)]. [(11,5), (13,5)]. [(0,4), (2,5)]. [(32,3), (33,8), (33,3), (34,8), (34,3), (35,8), (35,3), (36,8), (36,3)]. [(4,5), (4,3), (2,2), (1,1), (4,1), (6,2), (7,3), (7,5)]. [(6,7), (7,5), (8,2), (5,1), (5,0), (9,0), (10,2), (11,5), (10,7), (9,8)]. [(15,13), (14,11), (13,7), (13,5), (14,2), (12,1), (12,0), (17,0), (17,6), (19,8), (20,10), (20,12)]. [(17,6), (20,3), (18,2), (18,1), (23,1), (23,3), (22,5), (20,7)]. [(3,8), (2,8), (2,10), (3,10)]. [(4,9), (3,9), (3,11), (5,11), (5,10)]. [(4,11), (3,12), (3,14), (4,14)]. [(6,11), (5,11), (4,13), (4,15), (6,15), (8,14), (8,13)]. [(6,15), (6,18), (8,18)]. [(9,14), (8,15), (8,20), (12,20), (13,17), (12,16)]. [(11,20), (14,23), (15,22)]. [(14,17), (13,18), (14,21), (16,23), (18,22), (20,19), (20,18), (19,17)]. [(20,19), (22,21), (25,22), (26,20)]. [(21,16), (21,18), (24,20), (27,20), (27,17), (26,15), (25,13), (24,13)]. [(26,15), (29,15), (29,14)]. [(25,12), (25,13), (26,14), (30,14), (29,10), (27,9), (26,10)]. [(29,10), (30,10), (30,9)]. [(27,8), (27,9), (31,9), (30,6), (28,6)]. [(29,5), (29,6), (31,6), (31,4), (30,4)].

Now draw an eye like this ◖• around the point (1,6).

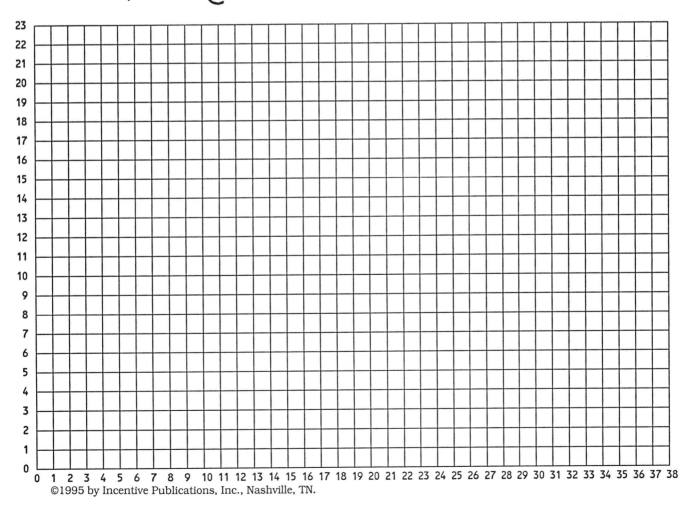

©1995 by Incentive Publications, Inc., Nashville, TN.

NAME_____

A Pyramid of Cubes

DIRECTIONS: Draw each of the configurations below in the appropriate grid blocks. Next to each configuration there is a list of grid blocks where the configuration is to be placed. You may use a colored pencil for the shaded areas.

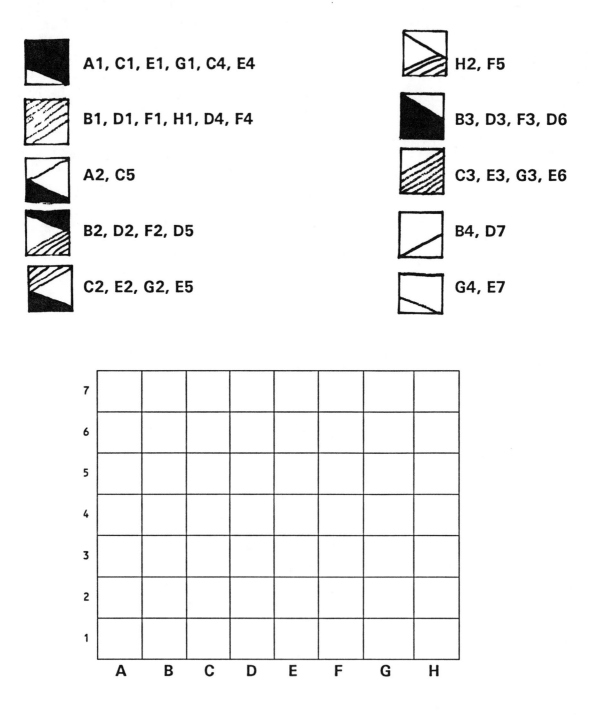

A1, C1, E1, G1, C4, E4

H2, F5

B1, D1, F1, H1, D4, F4

B3, D3, F3, D6

A2, C5

C3, E3, G3, E6

B2, D2, F2, D5

B4, D7

C2, E2, G2, E5

G4, E7

©1995 by Incentive Publications, Inc., Nashville, TN.

NAME

Chain

DIRECTIONS: Draw each of the configurations below in the appropriate grid blocks. Next to each configuration there is a list of grid blocks where the configuration is to be placed.

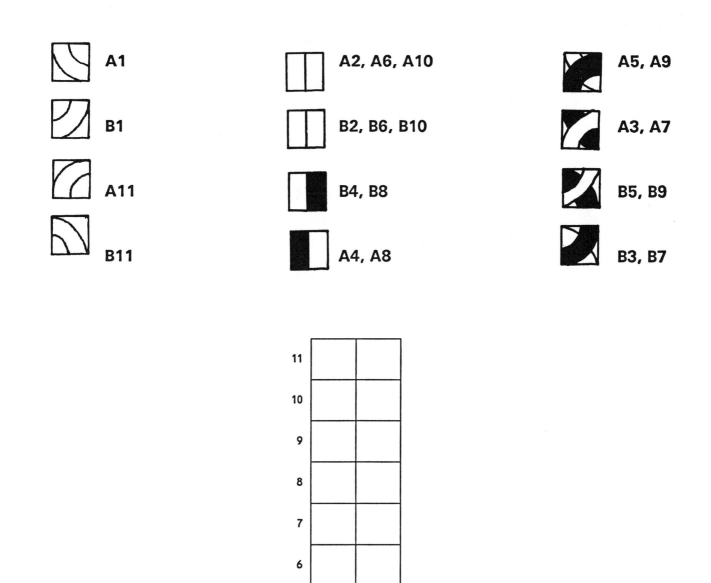

©1995 by Incentive Publications, Inc., Nashville, TN.

NAME_____

Circles and Squares

DIRECTIONS: Draw each of the configurations below in the appropriate grid blocks. Next to each configuration there is a list of grid blocks where the configuration is to be placed. You may use a colored pencil for the shaded areas.

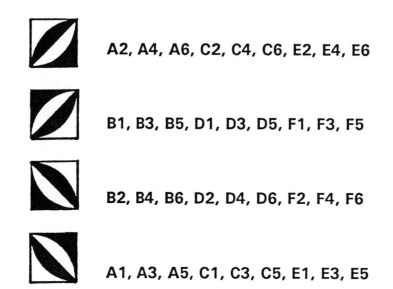

A2, A4, A6, C2, C4, C6, E2, E4, E6

B1, B3, B5, D1, D3, D5, F1, F3, F5

B2, B4, B6, D2, D4, D6, F2, F4, F6

A1, A3, A5, C1, C3, C5, E1, E3, E5

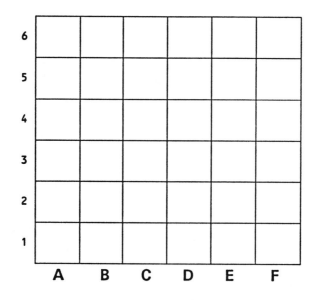

©1995 by Incentive Publications, Inc., Nashville, TN.

Graphing grid blocks

Something Familiar

DIRECTIONS: Draw each of the configurations below in the appropriate grid blocks. Next to each configuration there is a list of grid blocks where the configuration is to be placed.

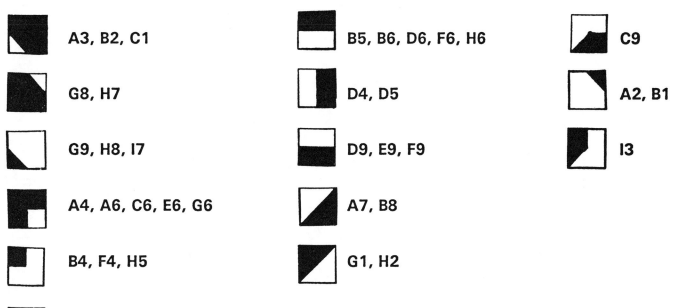

A3, B2, C1

B5, B6, D6, F6, H6

C9

G8, H7

D4, D5

A2, B1

G9, H8, I7

D9, E9, F9

I3

A4, A6, C6, E6, G6

A7, B8

B4, F4, H5

G1, H2

A5, E4, E5, F5, G4, G5, I4, I5, I6

B3, B7, C2, C3, C4, C5, C7, C8, D1, D2, D3, D7, D8, E1, E2, E3, E7, E8, F1, F2, F3, F7, F8, G2, G3, G7, H3, H4

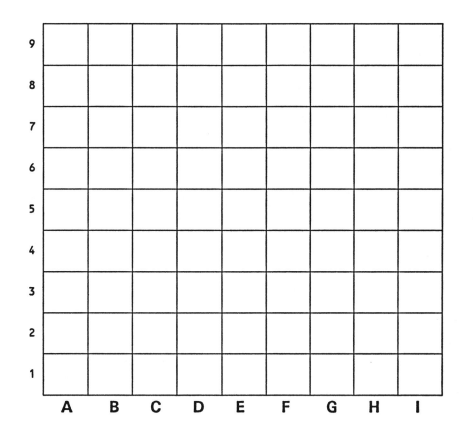

©1995 by Incentive Publications, Inc., Nashville, TN.

Reconstructing a puzzle

NAME_____

What insect appears ferocious as a caterpillar?

BACKGROUND INFORMATION: I am the largest of the butterflies in the United States. I can emit a very disagreeable odor if I'm bothered. There are several species of me in the United States. We have unusual names like "Tiger," "Black," and "Spicebush."

What am I? _____

DIRECTIONS: Draw each of the configurations below in the appropriate grid blocks. Above each configuration is listed the grid block where the configuration is to be placed.

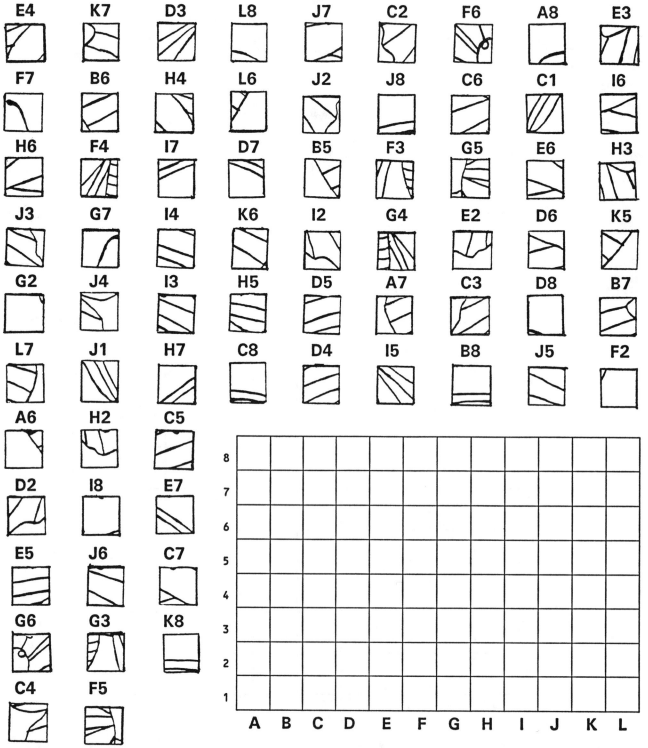

©1995 by Incentive Publications, Inc., Nashville, TN.

Reconstructing a puzzle

NAME_____

What is the oldest living reptile?

DIRECTIONS: Draw each of the configurations below in the appropriate grid blocks. The location of each grid block is given below each configuration.

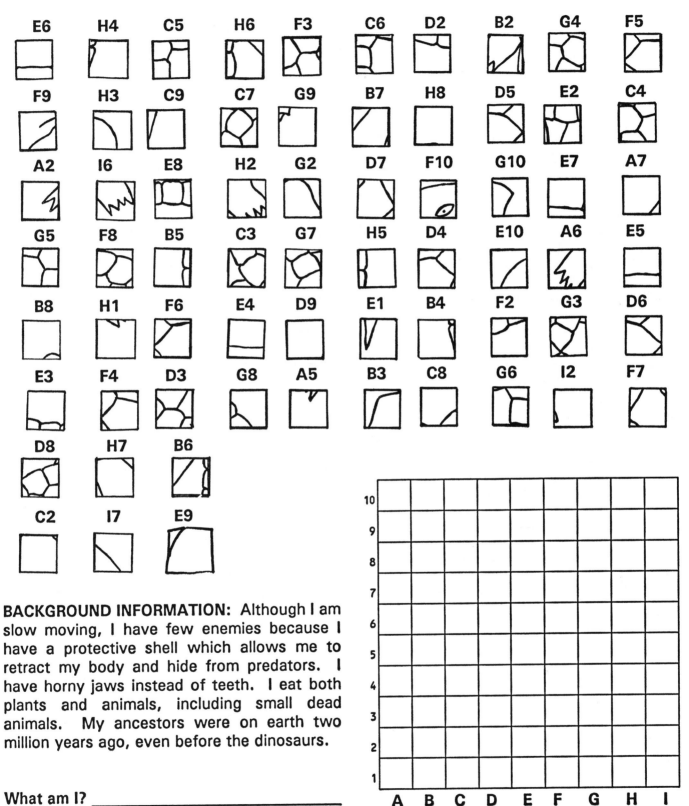

BACKGROUND INFORMATION: Although I am slow moving, I have few enemies because I have a protective shell which allows me to retract my body and hide from predators. I have horny jaws instead of teeth. I eat both plants and animals, including small dead animals. My ancestors were on earth two million years ago, even before the dinosaurs.

What am I? _____

©1995 by Incentive Publications, Inc., Nashville, TN.

Graphing positive and negative coordinates

NAME_____

Heart

DIRECTIONS: The heart is made of one continuous line. Graph the coordinates in the order given below. Use your ruler to draw your lines.

(0,0), (2,3), (5,3), (7,0), (7,-3), (0,-9), (-7,-3), (-7,0), (-5,3), (-2,3), (0,0)

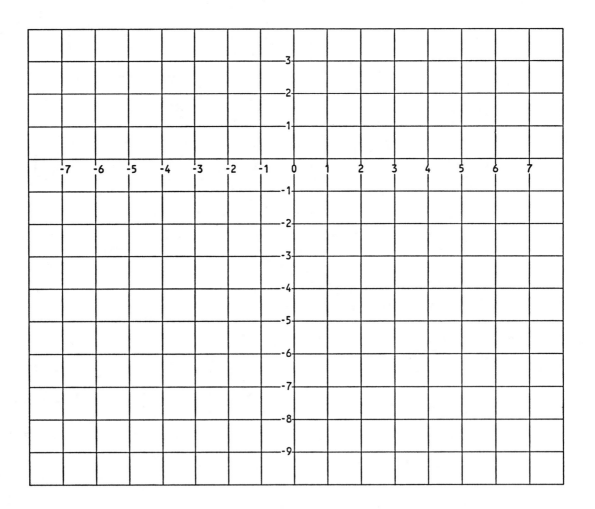

©1995 by Incentive Publications, Inc., Nashville, TN.

NAME_____

Satellite

DIRECTIONS: There are different types of satellites. Some are man-made and some are not. To find out what kind of a satellite I am, graph the coordinates in the order given below. This graph will be made of one continuous line.

(9,1), (9,-2), (6,1), (6,-2), (5,-2), (5,1), (2,1), (2,-2), (1,-2), (1,1), (-2,1), (-2,-2), (-3,-2),

(-3,1), (-5,-1), (-7,1), (-7,-2), (9,-2)

A Nine-Pointed Star

DIRECTIONS: The star is made of one continuous line. Use a ruler to draw your lines. The graph consists of the following positive and negative coordinates:

(3,5), (-1,-6), (-1,6), (3,-5), (-5,4), (6,-2), (-6,0), (6,2), (-5,-4), (3,5)

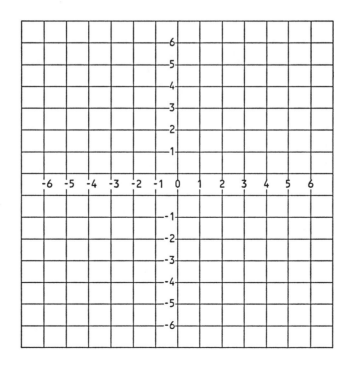

©1995 by Incentive Publications, Inc., Nashville, TN.

NAME_____

What amphibian enjoys singing?

DIRECTIONS: This graph has positive and negative coordinates. It is made up of 4 lines. The symbol [denotes the beginning of a line, and the symbol] denotes the end of a line. Graph the coordinates in the order given below.

[(3,0), (8,1), (9,1), (10,0), (7,-9), (9,-11), (6,-9), (8,-1), (0,-3), (-8,-1), (-6,-9), (-9,-11), (-7,-9), (-10,0), (-9,1), (-8,1), (-3,0)]. [(-2,-1), (-3,0), (-4,3), (-4,4), (-8,7), (-5,12), (-3,12), (-5,10), (-6,7), (-4,6), (-3,5)]. [(-4,6), (-2,10), (-1,11), (1,11), (2,10), (4,6)]. [(3,5), (4,6), (6,7), (5,10), (3,12), (5,12), (8,7), (4,4), (4,3), (3,0), (2,-1)].

Next draw a pair of eyes, like this ☉, around the points (-1,9) and (1,9).

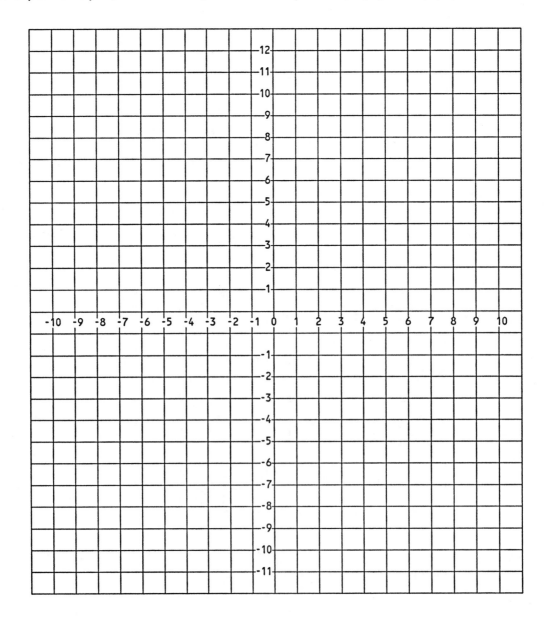

Answer to riddle: _____

©1995 by Incentive Publications, Inc., Nashville, TN.

NAME _____

Graphing positive and negative coordinates

What marsupial is known for its incredible speed and jumping power?

BACKGROUND INFORMATION: I am a marsupial that lives in Australia. My baby is called a joey and is nursed in my pouch. I am known for my incredible speed and also for my ability to jump.

What am I?

DIRECTIONS: This graph has positive and negative coordinates. It is made up of 5 lines. The symbol [denotes the beginning of a line, and the symbol] denotes the end of a line. Graph the coordinates in the order given below.

[(-8,2), (-9,4), (-9,7), (-11,7), (-11,8), (-9,10), (-8,10), (-6,12), (-7,10), (-5,11), (-6,10), (-6,7), (-5,5), (2,4), (5,2), (,-6), (16,-7), (19,-7), (21,-8), (7,-8), (4,-5), (2,-5) (1,-4)]. [(-8,4), (-7,3), (-9,0), (-8,-1), (-8,0), (-5,3), (-6,4)]. [(-7,1), (-4,-2), (-1,-4)]. [(2,2), (1,3), (0,3), (-2,1), (-2,0), (-1,-4), (-1,-7), (-4,-7), (-7,-8), (1,-8), (1,-4), (3,-3)]. [(2,-5), (2,-8), (1,-8)]. Next draw an eye, like this ⊙, around the point (-9,9).

©1995 by Incentive Publications, Inc., Nashville, TN.

NAME_____

GEOMETRIC EXTRAVAGANZA

DIRECTIONS: Using the perpendicular lines on the next page, connect the points on the vertical and horizontal axes in the order given. A small version of this activity is shown at the bottom of this page to help you get started. (Note: The numbers are on your vertical and horizontal lines in the smaller version, but not on your larger one. You may want to lightly pencil in the numbers on your larger perpendicular lines then erase them later.) The first number of each pair is always on the vertical axis.

[16,-1]   [15,-2]   [14,-3]   [13,-4]   [12,-5]   [11,-6]   [10,-7]   [9,-8]   [8,-9]
[7,-10]   [6,-11]   [5,-12]   [4,-13]   [3,-14]   [2,-15]   [1,-16]

[-16,-1]   [-15,-2]   [-14,-3]   [-13,-4]   [-12,-5]   [-11,-6]   [-10,-7]   [-9,-8]   [-8,-9]
[-7,-10]   [-6,-11]   [-5,-12]   [-4,-13]   [-3,-14]   [-2,-15]   [-1,-16]

[16,1]   [15,2]   [14,3]   [13,4]   [12,5]   [11,6]   [10,7]   [9,8]   [8,9]   [7,10]
[6,11]   [5,12]   [4,13]   [3,14]   [2,15]   [1,16]

[-16,1]   [-15,2]   [-14,3]   [-13,4]   [-12,5]   [-11,6]   [-10,7]   [-9,8]   [-8,9]
[-7,10]   [-6,11]   [-5,12]   [-4,13]   [-3,14]   [-2,15]   [-1,16]

Color and shade your drawing.

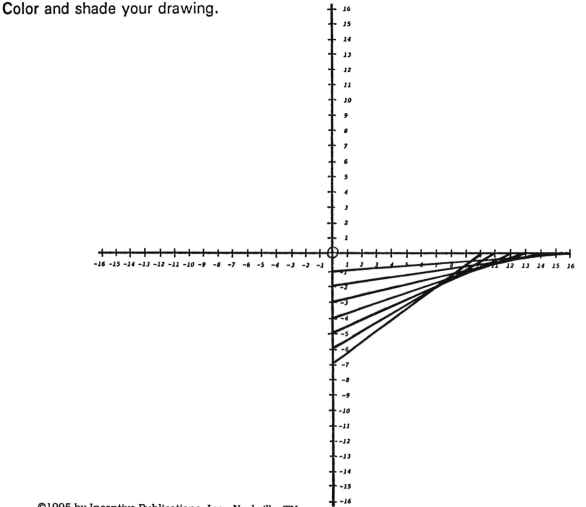

©1995 by Incentive Publications, Inc., Nashville, TN.

Graphing coordinates on perpendicular lines

NAME_____

GEOMETRIC EXTRAVAGANZA

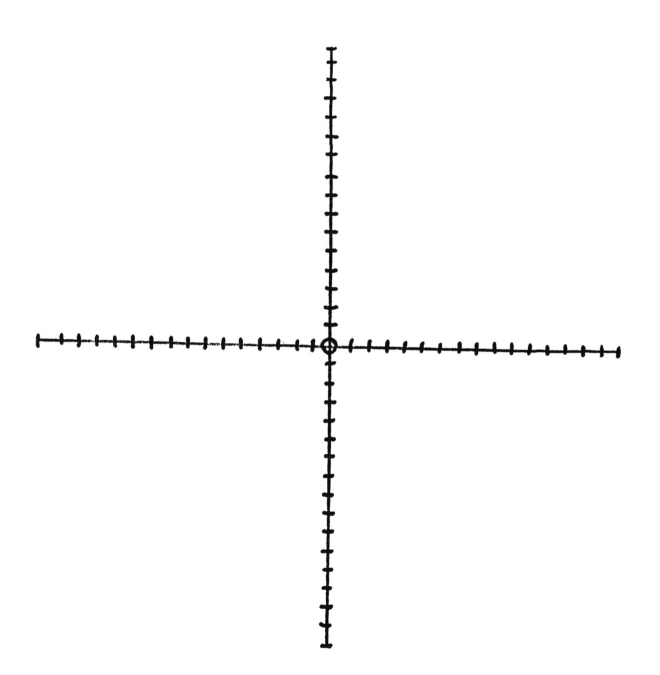

©1995 by Incentive Publications, Inc., Nashville, TN.

NAME_____

Selling Apples

DIRECTIONS: Use the pictograph below to answer the questions

One day when Josh was helping his father sell apples at a roadside stand, he decided to make a pictograph of the bushels of apples sold that day. Here is what he did:

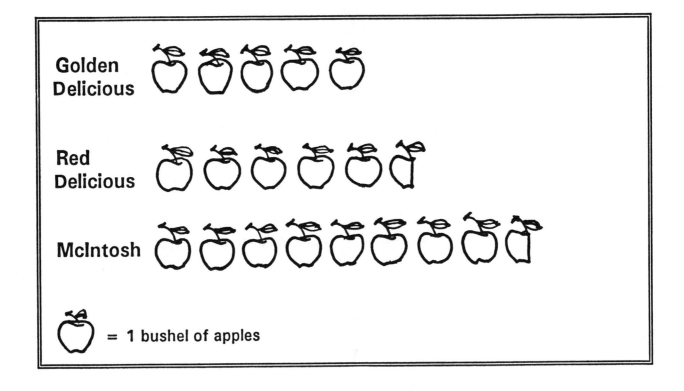

1.   Of what type of apple did they sell the most?_____

2.   How many bushels of each type of apple were sold?

        _____bushels of Golden Delicious

        _____bushels of Red Delicious

        _____bushels of McIntosh

3.   If Red delicious apples sold for $10 per bushel, Golden delicious for $9 per bushel, and McIntosh for $8 per bushel, what were the total sales for that day?

©1995 by Incentive Publications, Inc., Nashville, TN.

NAME_____

Planets and their Moons

DIRECTIONS: Circle the correct answer.

1. Which planet besides Earth has only one moon?

    a) Venus   b) Mars   c)   Pluto

2. Which planets have no moons?

    a) Neptune and Pluto   b) Venus and Mercury   c) Venus and Pluto

3. Which planet has the most number of moons?

    a) Jupiter   b) Saturn   c) Uranus

4. How many moons does Jupiter have?

    a) 9   b) 12   c) 17

5. How many moons does Uranus have?

    a) 8   b) 10   c) 15

6. How many more moons does Neptune have than Pluto?

    a) 1   b) 2   c) 3

©1995 by Incentive Publications, Inc., Nashville, TN.

NAME _____

Average Life Span of Some Familiar Animals

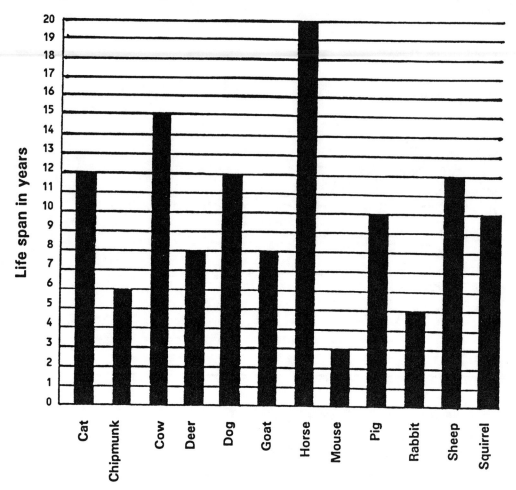

DIRECTIONS: Answer the questions by reading the bar graph.

1. Which of the animals above has the longest life span? _____

2. Which of the animals above has the shortest life span? _____

3. What other animals have the same average life span as a cat? _____

   _____

4. Which animal lives 3 times longer than a rabbit? _____

5. Which lives longer, a squirrel or a chipmunk?   _____

   By how many years? _____

6. Which of the animals above have a life span less than that of a chipmunk? _____

   _____

7. Put the animals in order from the longest life span to the shortest life span. Write the life span of
   each animal by its name. **Example:** __horse - 20 years__

©1995 by Incentive Publications, Inc., Nashville, TN.

NAME_____

Our Missions to the Moon

Between July of 1969, and December of 1972, there were 7 missions to the moon. The bar graph below shows how long each mission remained on the moon.

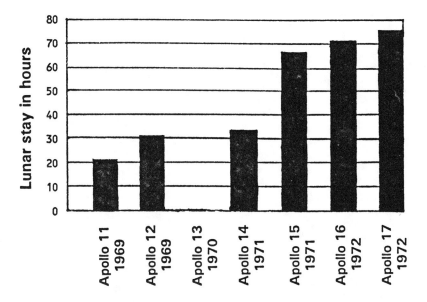

DIRECTIONS: Answer the following questions by reading the bar graph.

1. There was one unsuccessful lunar mission. One oxygen tank ruptured and the crew aborted its mission and came back to earth safely. Which mission was it? _____

2. Of the successful missions, which mission had the shortest lunar stay? _____

3. Which mission had the longest lunar stay? _____

4. How many lunar missions were launched in 1972? _____

5. About how many hours did the crew of the first lunar mission spend on the moon? _____

6. How many more hours did Apollo 17 stay on the moon than Apollo 11? _____

7. What is the total number of hours spent on the moon by all of the Apollo missions? _____

8. Over how many years did all of the Apollo missions together span? _____

©1995 by Incentive Publications, Inc., Nashville, TN.

NAME_____

Highest Mountains

The graph below shows the highest mountains in each of the seven continents.

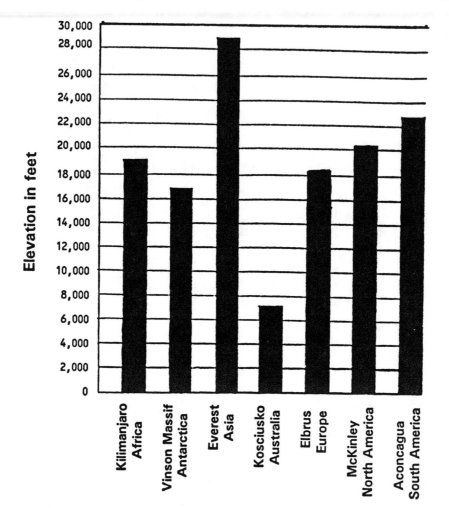

DIRECTIONS: Answer the questions by reading the bar graph.

1. Which mountain is about 12,000 feet higher than Mt. Kosciusko? _____

2. What is the elevation of Mt. McKinley to the nearest thousand? _____

3. Which is the highest mountain in the Americas? _____

4. Which mountain is about 4 times as high as Mt. Kosciusko? _____

5. Which continent(s) has (have) no mountains above 10,000 feet in elevation? _____
_____

6. How many continents have mountains higher than the highest mountain in Europe? _____

©1995 by Incentive Publications, Inc., Nashville, TN.

NAME_____

Average Distance of Planets From the Sun

DIRECTIONS: Answer the following questions by reading the graph on the following page. Circle the correct answer.

1.   Which planet is the closest to the sun?

   a) Venus   b) Mars   c) Mercury   d) Pluto

2.   The average distance of Earth from the sun is:

   a) 93 miles   b) 93,000 miles   c) 93,000,000 miles

3.   How far is Uranus from the sun?

   a) 893 million miles   b) 1,797 million miles   c) 2,815 million miles

4.   How many planets are less than 100 million miles from Earth?

   a) 1   b) 2   c) 3   d) 4

5.   How many planets are less than 500 million miles from Uranus?

   a) 0   b) 1   c) 2   d) 3

6.   Which planet is twice the distance of Saturn from the sun?

   a) Uranus   b) Neptune   c) Pluto

7.   The average distance of Pluto from the sun is _____ times the average distance of Mercury from the sun.

   a) 10   b) 100   c) 1,000

©1995 by Incentive Publications, Inc., Nashville, TN.

NAME_____

Average Distance of Planets From the Sun

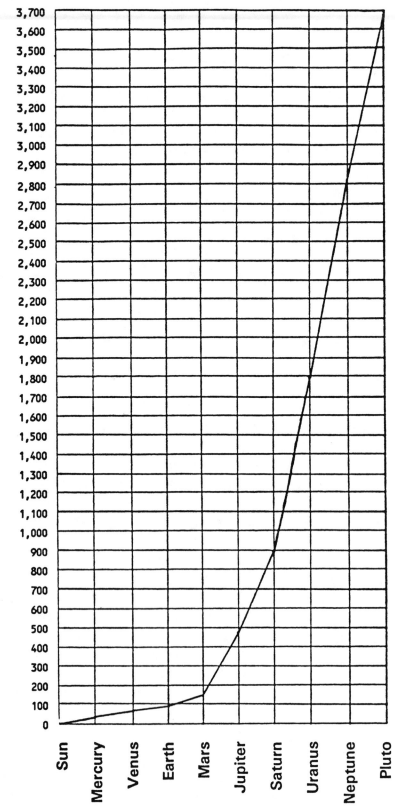

©1995 by Incentive Publications, Inc., Nashville, TN.

NAME_____

68

Elevation and the Boiling Point of Water

The graph below shows the relationship between elevation and the boiling point of water. The boiling point of water is 100°C only at sea level. Circle the correct answer.

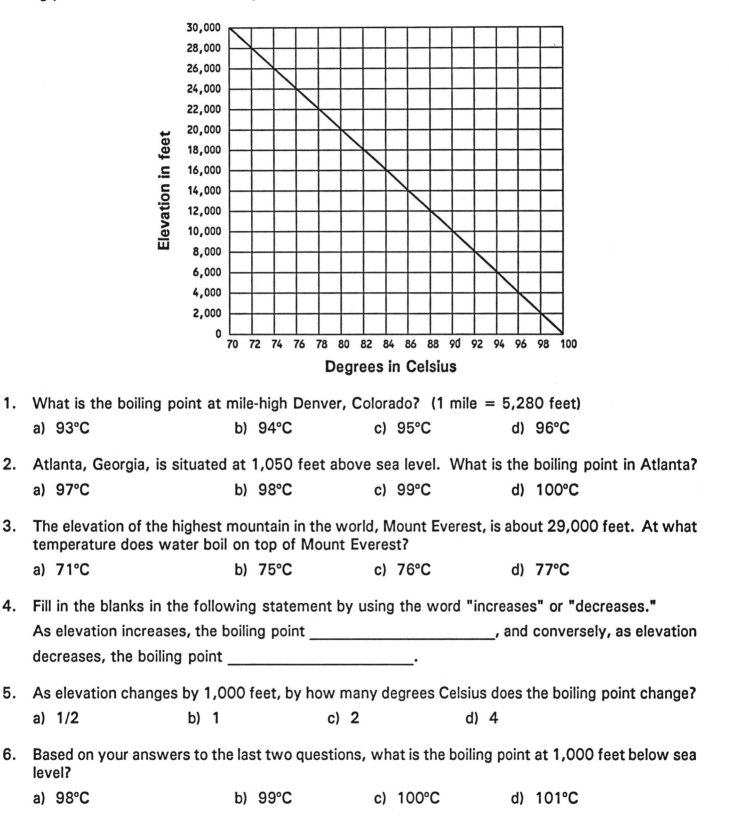

1. What is the boiling point at mile-high Denver, Colorado? (1 mile = 5,280 feet)

    a) 93°C   b) 94°C   c) 95°C   d) 96°C

2. Atlanta, Georgia, is situated at 1,050 feet above sea level. What is the boiling point in Atlanta?

    a) 97°C   b) 98°C   c) 99°C   d) 100°C

3. The elevation of the highest mountain in the world, Mount Everest, is about 29,000 feet. At what temperature does water boil on top of Mount Everest?

    a) 71°C   b) 75°C   c) 76°C   d) 77°C

4. Fill in the blanks in the following statement by using the word "increases" or "decreases."

    As elevation increases, the boiling point _____, and conversely, as elevation

    decreases, the boiling point _____.

5. As elevation changes by 1,000 feet, by how many degrees Celsius does the boiling point change?

    a) 1/2   b) 1   c) 2   d) 4

6. Based on your answers to the last two questions, what is the boiling point at 1,000 feet below sea level?

    a) 98°C   b) 99°C   c) 100°C   d) 101°C

©1995 by Incentive Publications, Inc., Nashville, TN.

NAME_____

CREATING GRAPHS

DIRECTIONS: Convert one of the tables below into either a bar, line or pictograph.

Underwater Vehicular Tunnels in the U.S.A.

NAME OF TUNNEL	LOCATION	WATERWAY	LENGTH IN FEET
Holland	New York, NY	Hudson River	8,557
Lincoln	New York, NY	Hudson River	8,216
Baltimore Harbor	Baltimore, MD	Patapsco River	7,650
Fort McHenry	Baltimore, MD	Baltimore Harbor	7,200
Sumner	Boston, MA	Boston Harbor	5,650
Callahan	Boston, MA	Boston Harbor	5,046

Notable Volcanic Eruptions

VOLCANO	YEAR	DEATHS
Krakatau, Indonesia	1883	35,000
Mt. Pelée, Martinique	1902	30,000
Nevado del Ruiz, Colombia	1985	23,000
Mt. Etna, Sicily	1669	20,000
Mt. Vesuvius, Italy	79 A.D.	16,000

YEAR	PLAYER	NL TEAM	PCT	PLAYER	AL TEAM	PCT
1993	A. Galarraga	Rockies	.370	J. Olerud	Blue Jays	.363
1992	G. Sheffield	Padres	.330	E. Martinez	Mariners	.343
1991	T. Pendleton	Braves	.319	J. Franco	Rangers	.342
1990	W. McGee	Cardinals	.335	G. Brett	Royals	.329

Largest Cities (based on population projection for the year 2000)

CITY	COUNTRY	PROJECTED POPULATION
Tokyo-Yokohama	Japan	29,971,000
Mexico City	Mexico	27,872,000
Sao Paulo	Brazil	25,354,000
Seoul	South Korea	21,976,000
New York City	United States	14,648,000

©1995 by Incentive Publications, Inc., Nashville, TN.

NAME_____

GRAPHING PROJECT - DECISION MAKING

Several alternatives that I will consider using as the topic for my graphing project are:

1._____   4._____

2._____   5._____

3._____   6._____

Questions that I will ask to help me choose a topic are:

1._____

2._____

3._____

4._____

5._____

My choice for a topic for my graphing project is:

_____

The many, varied reasons I chose this topic are:

1._____

2._____

3._____

4._____

5._____

©1995 by Incentive Publications, Inc., Nashville, TN.

Using higher order thinking skills for a graphing project   NAME_____

GRAPHING PROJECT - PLANNING

1. Write a brief description of the graphing project: _____

_____

_____

_____

_____

2. The materials I will need to complete the project are:

_____   _____

_____   _____

_____   _____

_____   _____

_____   _____

3. List the steps in order needed to complete the graph:

_____

_____

_____

_____

_____

_____

_____

4. List the problems that might occur:

_____

_____

_____

_____

_____

_____

_____

©1995 by Incentive Publications, Inc., Nashville, TN.

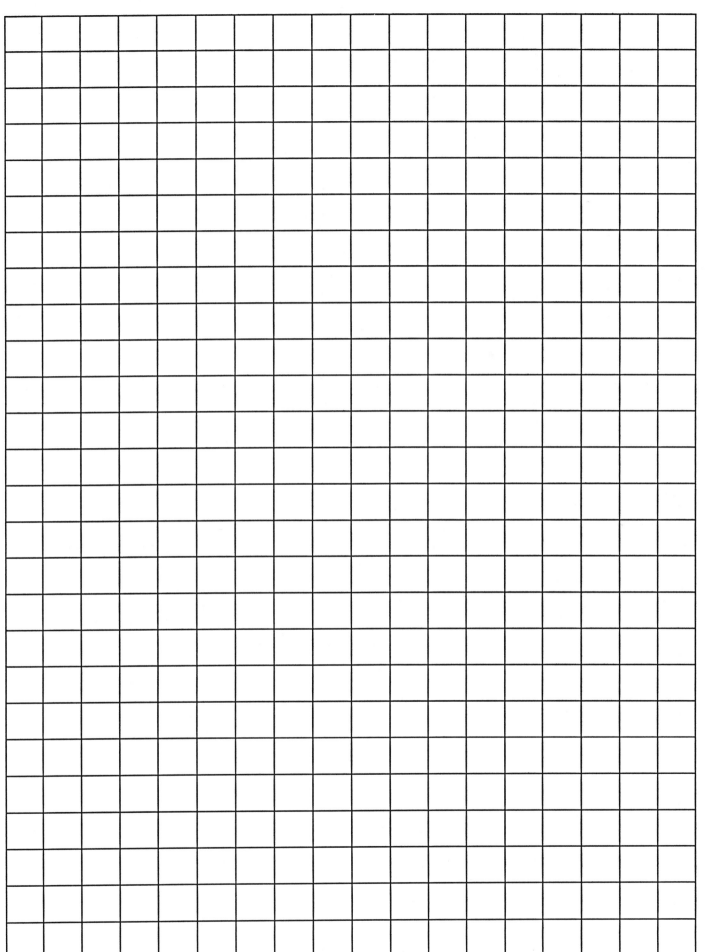

©1995 by Incentive Publications, Inc., Nashville, TN.

73

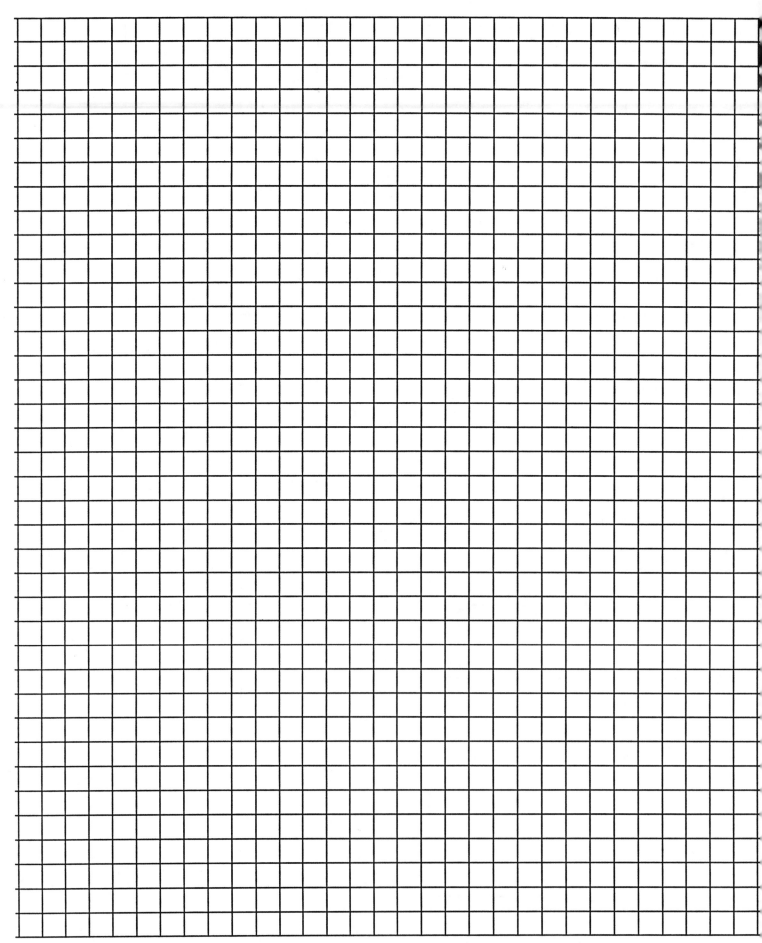

©1995 by Incentive Publications, Inc., Nashville, TN.

BRAIN CHALLENGERS:

GEOMETRY   AND   GRAPHING

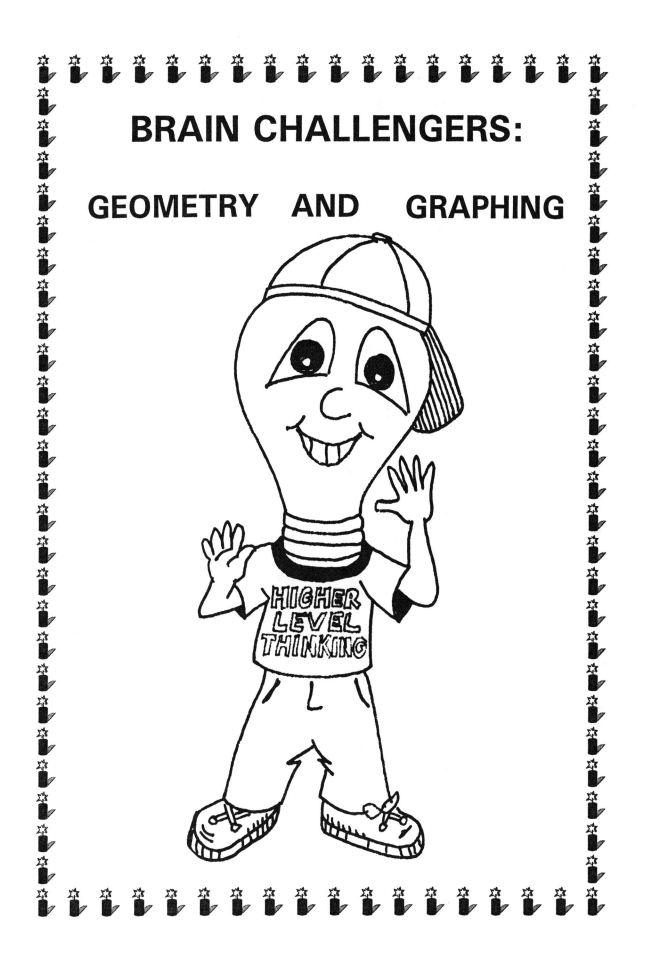

©1995 by Incentive Publications, Inc., Nashville, TN.

NAME_____

GEOMETRIC PUZZLES WITH TANGRAMS

DIRECTIONS: Many geometric figures can be constructed with tangrams. Some figures will **require all seven pieces**, while other figures will require less. Students will need a set of the seven tangram pieces given below. (The pieces must be cut carefully and accurately in order to construct the geometric figures. You may want to laminate the pieces.)

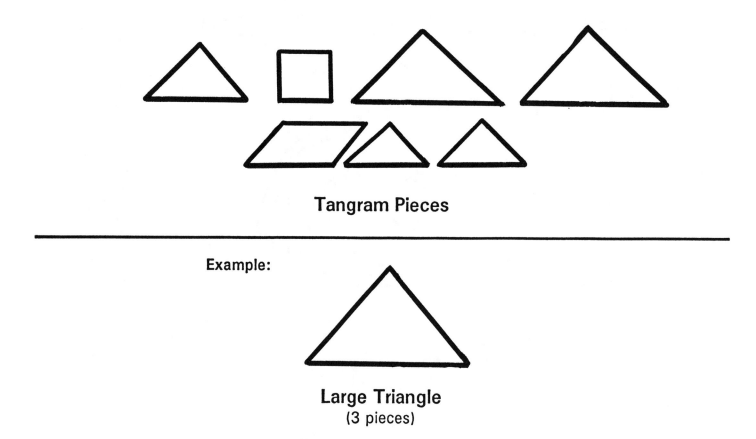

Tangram Pieces

Example:

Large Triangle
(3 pieces)

The three correct pieces to use turn out to be:

SOLUTION: Draw in correct lines on the triangle below.

©1995 by Incentive Publications, Inc., Nashville, TN.

Using tangrams to construct geometric figures

NAME_____

GEOMETRIC PUZZLES WITH TANGRAMS WORKSHEET

DIRECTIONS: Use the number of pieces indicated and when you have found the solution with your Tangram pieces, draw in the lines to show how the pieces fit.

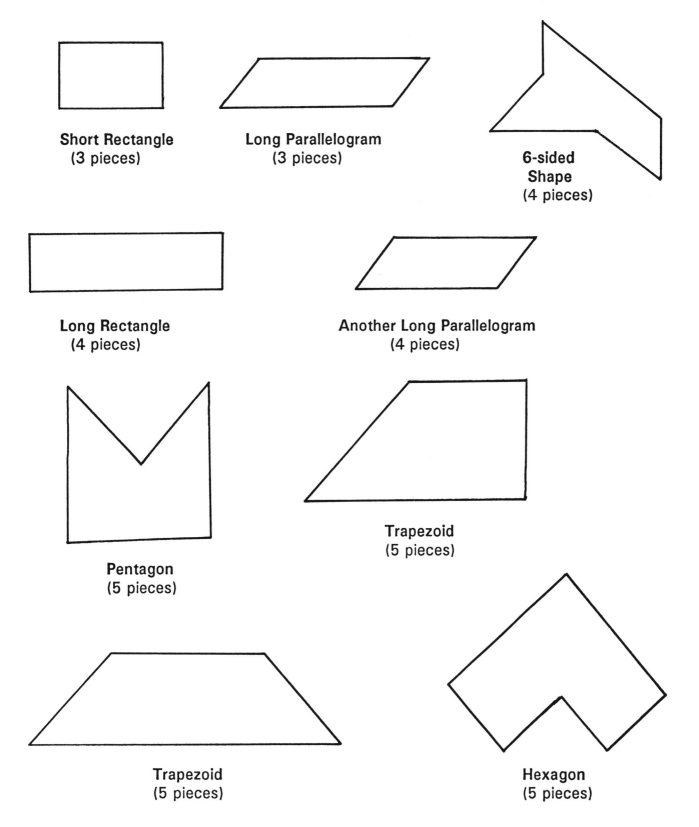

Short Rectangle
(3 pieces)

Long Parallelogram
(3 pieces)

6-sided Shape
(4 pieces)

Long Rectangle
(4 pieces)

Another Long Parallelogram
(4 pieces)

Pentagon
(5 pieces)

Trapezoid
(5 pieces)

Trapezoid
(5 pieces)

Hexagon
(5 pieces)

©1995 by Incentive Publications, Inc., Nashville, TN.

NAME_____

Octahedron Match

BACKGROUND INFORMATION: This is a picture of an octahedron. It has **8** faces. All of its faces are regular triangles.

For each face of an octahedron there is a face directly opposite it. The drawings below are all different views of the same octahedron.

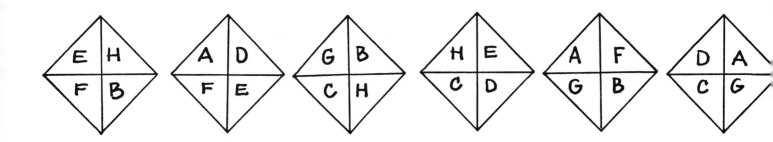

Which face lies directly opposite:

Face D? _____   Face C? _____

Face F? _____   Face A? _____

Face G? _____   Face H? _____

Face B? _____   Face E? _____

©1995 by Incentive Publications, Inc., Nashville, TN.

NAME_____

Remainder Math - Part I
Steps 1 & 2

In the first example a circle will be divided into **18** equal parts. The points marked on the circle will be called C numbers for "circumference" numbers.

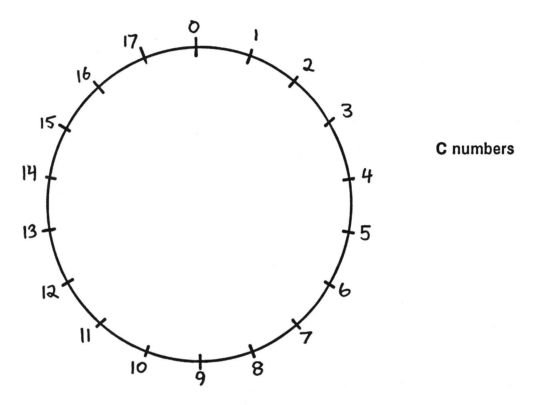

C numbers

Make a table with all the C numbers across the top:

C	0	1	2	3	4	5	6	7	8	9	10	11	12	13	14	15	16	17

©1995 by Incentive Publications, Inc., Nashville, TN.

NAME_____

Remainder Math - Part I
Steps 3 & 4

For each C number, there will be a corresponding R number, or "remainder" number. The first set of R numbers will be completed as follows:

Step 3 To each C number add the number 5 and then divide the sum by 18 (our total circumference numbers). The R number (or remainder number) will be placed under the C number used in the table. *Remember, only use the <u>remainder</u> from each division problem. [Formula: (C + 5) ÷ 18 = R]

Example: For C = 0   C + 5 = 0 + 5 = 5
Dividing by 18, we get 5 ÷ 18 = 0 R.5

$$18\overline{)5}\begin{array}{c}0\ \text{R.5}\\ \underline{0}\\ 5\end{array}$$

Place the R number 5 under the C number used, 0.

C	0	1	2	3	4	5	6	7	8	9	10	11	12	13	14	15	16	17
R	5																	

Another example:

For C = 15   C + 5 = 15 + 5 = 20
Dividing by 18, we get 20 ÷ 18 = 1 R.2
R = 2 and therefore C = 15 → R = 2

$$18\overline{)20}\begin{array}{c}1\ \text{R.2}\\ \underline{18}\\ 2\end{array}$$

Complete the table using this same formula: (C + 5) ÷ 18 = R

Step 4 On the circle, connect each C number with its corresponding R number by drawing a straight line from one to the other.

Example:

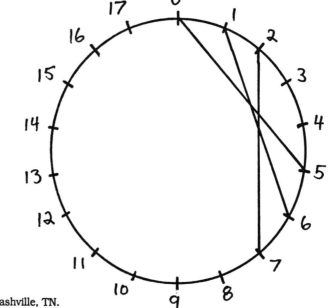

©1995 by Incentive Publications, Inc., Nashville, TN.

Combining geometry and art

Remainder Math - Part II
Circles 1 - 4

DIRECTIONS: Use the same directions described in Part I of Remainder Math to complete the circles given below. You will need to make your own table on another sheet of paper. Then, using the formulas given for each circle, connect each C number with its corresponding R number by drawing a straight line from one to the other.

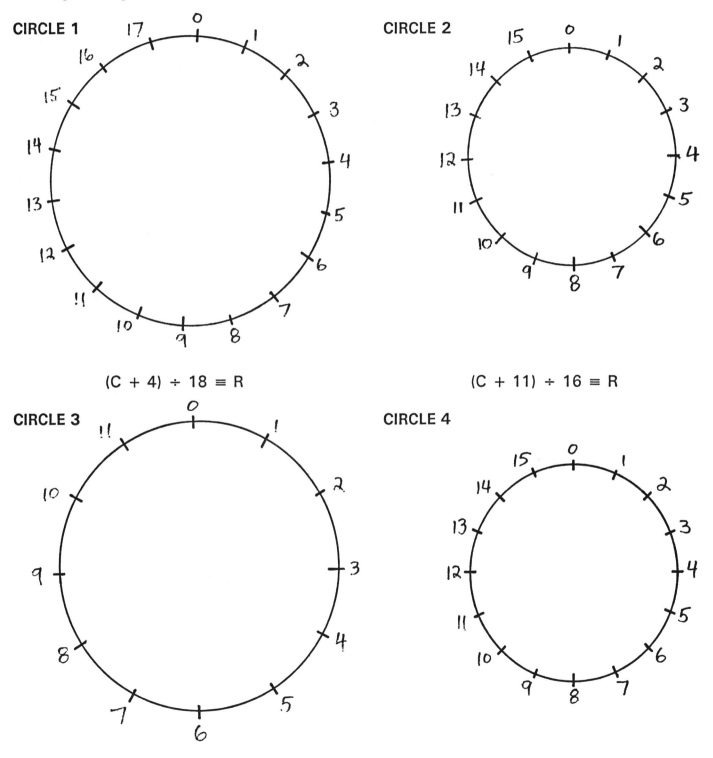

CIRCLE 1

$(C + 4) \div 18 \equiv R$

CIRCLE 2

$(C + 11) \div 16 \equiv R$

CIRCLE 3

$(C + 4) \div 12 \equiv R$

CIRCLE 4

$[(C \times 6) + 3] \div 16 \equiv R$

©1995 by Incentive Publications, Inc., Nashville, TN.

NAME_____

Remainder Math - Part II
Circles 5 - 7

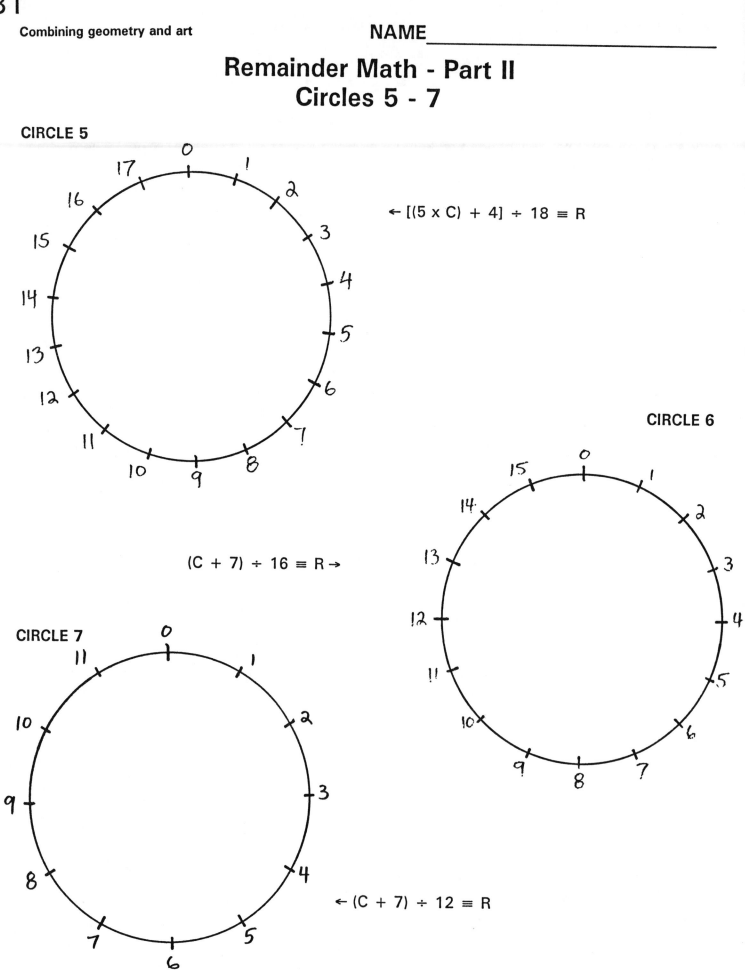

CIRCLE 5

← [(5 x C) + 4] ÷ 18 ≡ R

(C + 7) ÷ 16 ≡ R →

CIRCLE 6

CIRCLE 7

← (C + 7) ÷ 12 ≡ R

©1995 by Incentive Publications, Inc., Nashville, TN.

Devising formulas for circles

Remainder Math - Part III

DIRECTIONS: By making up your own formula, you can do your own remainder math design. For the circles below, devise your own formula and write this formula on the line provided under each circle.

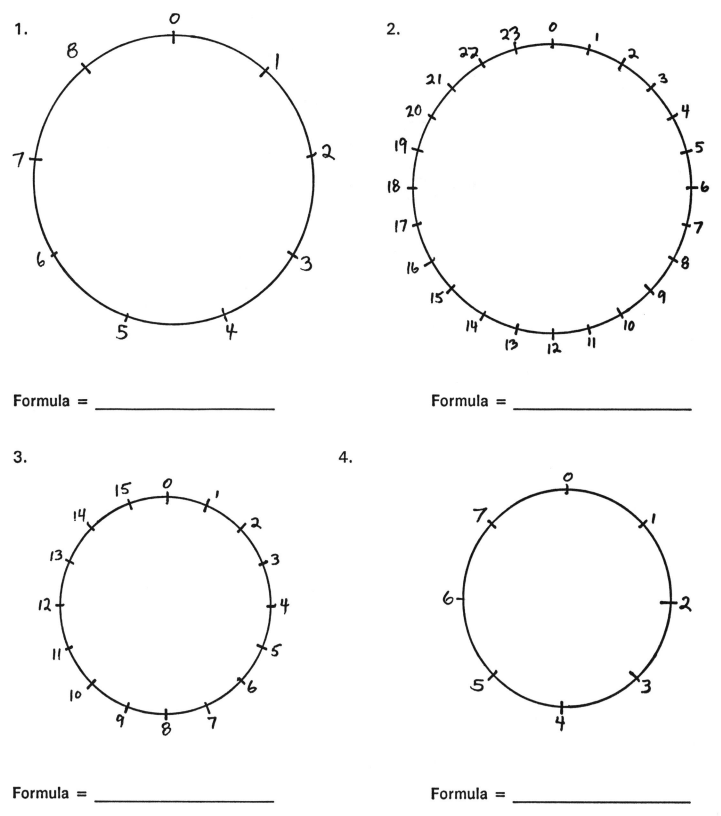

1.

Formula = _____

2.

Formula = _____

3.

Formula = _____

4.

Formula = _____

©1995 by Incentive Publications, Inc., Nashville, TN.

Enlarging a design by doubling the dimensions

NAME_____

PROPORTIONAL DRAWINGS

DIRECTIONS: Make an enlargement of the small drawing below on the large grid. A line on the small grid should be matched with a corresponding position on the large grid. Your enlarged drawing will be four times the size of the one on the small grid.

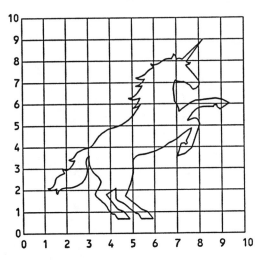

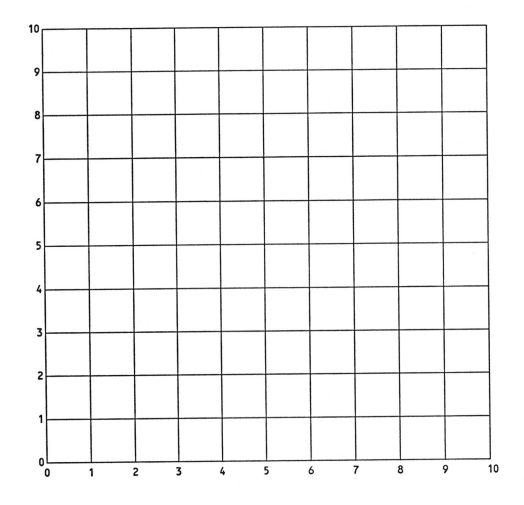

©1995 by Incentive Publications, Inc., Nashville, TN.

PROPORTIONAL DRAWINGS

DIRECTIONS: Make an enlargement of the small drawing below on the large grid. A line on the small grid should be matched with a corresponding position on the large grid. Your enlarged drawing will be four times the size of the one on the small grid.

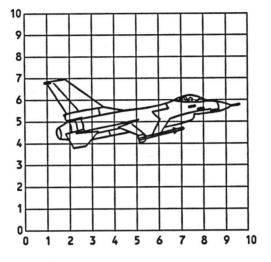

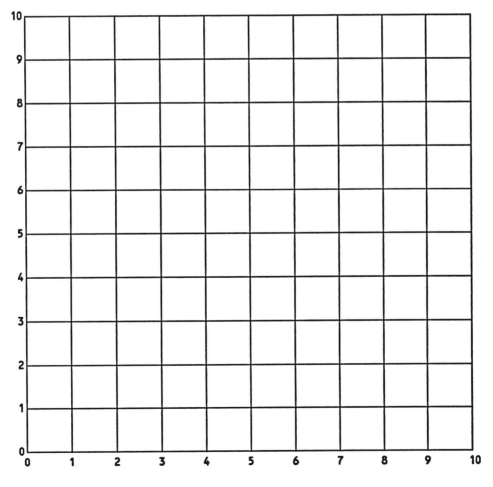

©1995 by Incentive Publications, Inc., Nashville, TN.

NAME_____

What bird of prey keeps the same nest throughout its life?

BACKGROUND INFORMATION: I am a bird of prey. I keep the same nest throughout my life. My nest weighs as much as a ton.

What am I? _____

DIRECTIONS: This graph is made up of several lines. The symbol [denotes the beginning of a line, and the symbol] denotes the end of a line. Graph the coordinates in the order given below.

[(20,9), (17,9), (14,10), (10,12), (5,17), (3,18), (1,18), (3,19), (1,19), (0,18), (0,19), (1,20), (2,20), (3,22), (5,22), (7,21), (10,20), (10,22), (9,24), (6,27), (1,30), (1,33), (3,39), (5,43), (7,46), (9,47), (9,46)].

[(6,42), (9,46), (10,47), (12,48), (12,47)]. [(8,42), (12,47), (14,47), (14,46)].

[(9,41), (14,46), (16,46), (15,44)]. [(11,41), (15,44), (17,44), (16,43)].

[(12,40), (16,43), (18,43), (17,42)]. [(12,38), (17,42), (18,41), (16,39)].

[(12,36), (16,39), (17,39), (17,38)]. [(13,34), (17,38), (18,38), (18,37), (17,36)].

[(14,33), (17,36), (18,36), (18,35), (17,34)]. [(15,32), (17,34), (18,34), (18,33)].

[(15,30), (18,33), (20,33), (19,32)]. [(17,30), (19,32), (21,32), (20,31)].

[(18,29), (20,31), (22,31), (21,30)]. [(18,28), (21,30), (23,30), (22,29)].

[(19,27), (22,29), (24,29), (23,28)]. [(19,26), (23,28), (24,28), (23,27)].

[(19,25), (23,27), (25,26), (23,25)]. [(19,24), (23,25), (25,25), (23,24)].

[(19,23), (23,24), (25,23), (24,22)]. [(19,22), (24,22), (25,21), (23,21)].

[(19,21), (23,21), (24,20), (23,20)]. [(19,20), (23,20), (24,19), (22,19)].

[(19,19), (22,19), (24,18), (25,17), (23,17)]. [(19,18), (23,17), (24,16), (22,16)].

[(19,17), (22,16), (24,14), (22,14)]. [(18,17), (22,14), (22,13), (18,16)].

[(23,29), (27,33), (33,36), (37,36), (38,35), (33,35)]. [(36,35), (37,34), (32,34)].

[(35,34), (36,33), (31,33)]. [(35,33), (36,32), (31,32)]. [(34,32), (35,31), (30,31)].

[(33,31), (34,30), (30,30)]. [(32,30), (33,29), (29,29)].

[(32,29), (33,28), (29,28)]. [(31,28), (32,27), (28,27)].

[(30,27), (31,26), (27,26)]. [(30,26), (31,25), (27,25)].

[(29,25), (30,24), (26,24)]. [(29,24), (30,23), (26,23)].

[(28,23), (29,22), (26,22)]. [(28,22), (29,21), (26,21)].

[(27,21), (28,20), (25,20)]. [(26,20), (27,19), (25,19), (26,18), (24,18)].

[(24,17), (37,6), (36,5), (35,5), (34,4), (33,4), (32,3), (31,3), (30,2) (29,2), (28,1), (27,1), (26,0), (25,0), (21,8), (20,9), (18,12)].

[(17,9), (18,6), (17,5), (13,4), (14,3), (14,4), (16,4), (14,3), (15,2), (15,3), (18,4), (19,4), (19,3), (18,2), (19,2), (20,3), (20,4), (19,5), (20,6), (21,8)].

[(23,7), (27,1)]. [(24,9), (29,2)]. [(26,9), (31,3)]. [(27,11), (33,4)]. [(29,11), (35,5)].

Now draw an eye, like this ☉, around the point (5,20).

©1995 by Incentive Publications, Inc., Nashville, TN.

What bird of prey keeps the same nest throughout its life? NAME_____

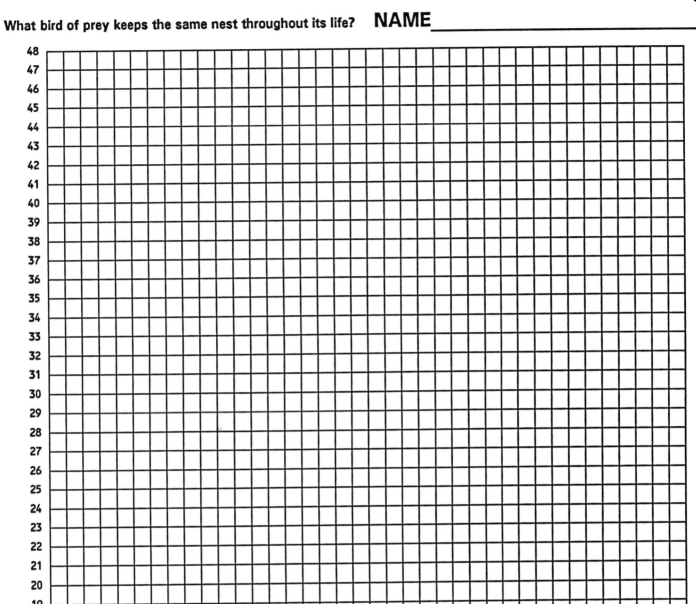
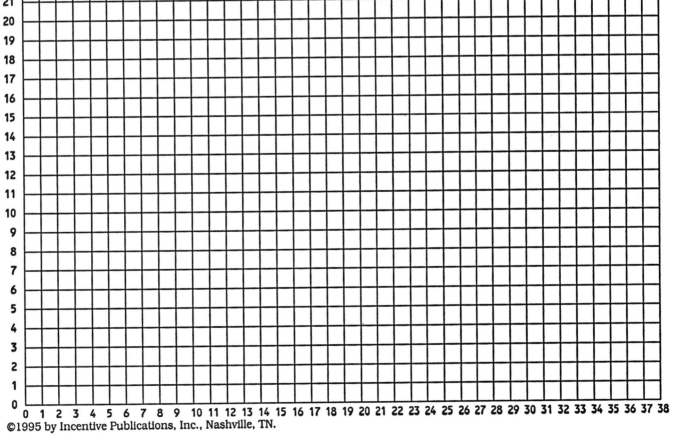

©1995 by Incentive Publications, Inc., Nashville, TN.

Graphing on an uneven grid

NAME_____

Space Shuttle

DIRECTIONS: This graph is made up of several lines. The symbol [denotes the beginning of a line, and the symbol] denotes the end of a line. Graph the coordinates in the order given below.

[(15,26), (19,26), (17,27), (15,26)]. [(15,21), (16,21), (16,22), (15,22), (15,21)].

[(18,21), (19,21), (19,22), (18,22), (18,21)]. [(5,16), (6,16), (6,17), (5,17), (5,16)].

[(13,23), (13,15), (10,15), (3,10), (2,8), (12,8), (12,7), (1,7), (2,11), (5,13), (7,14), (9,15), (10,17), (11,19), (13,23), (13,24), (15,25), (19,25), (21,24), (21,23), (23,19), (24,17), (25,16), (27,14), (28,14), (28,16), (27,16), (27,14), (29,13), (32,11), (33,7), (22,7), (22,8), (32,8), (31,10), (24,15), (21,15), (21,23), (19,23), (19,24), (15,24), (15,23), (13,23)].

At this point shade all the areas bounded by all of the lines above.

Now continue making the following lines:

[(5,13), (5,27), (8,29), (10,27), (10,17)]. [(5,27), (10,27)]. [(5,25), (10,25)]. [(5,21), (10,21)].

[(5,18), (10,18)]. [(5,14), (7,14)]. [(24,17), (24,27), (26,29), (29,27), (29,13)]. [(24,27), (29,27)].

[(24,25), (29,25)]. [(24,21), (29,21)]. [(24,18), (29,18)]. [(27,14), (29,14)].

[(11,19), (11,29), (13,30), (17,31), (21,30), (23,29), (23,19)]. [(11,28), (23,28)]. [(13,24), (15,26)].

[(19,26), (21,24)]. [(13,21), (21,21)]. [(13,20), (21,20)]. [(13,17), (21,17)]. [(13,14), (21,14)].

[(13,12), (21,12)]. [(13,11), (21,11)]. [(17,21), (17,12)]. [(13,15), (13,11)]. [(21,15), (21,11)].

[(1,7), (0,6), (5,5), (12,4), (12,9), (13,11)]. [(16,11), (17,9), (18,11)].

[(33,7), (34,6), (29,5), (22,4), (22,9), (21,11)]. [(17,9), (17,4)].

[(12,4), (13,3), (16,3), (17,4), (18,3), (21,3), (22,4)]. [(14,3), (12,1), (17,1), (15,3)].

[(19,3), (17,1), (22,1), (20,3)]. [(16,3), (15,2), (19,2), (18,3)].

[(29,5), (29,1), (30,0), (22,0), (24,1), (24,4)]. Extend this line about $\frac{1}{32}$" so it meets the line above it.

[(5,5), (5,1), (4,0), (12,0), (10,1), (10,4)]. Extend this line as you did on the right-hand side.

[(5,1), (10,1)]. [(5,3), (10,3)]. [(24,1), (29,1)]. [(24,3), (29,3)].

©1995 by Incentive Publications, Inc., Nashville, TN.

Graphing on an uneven grid

Space Shuttle

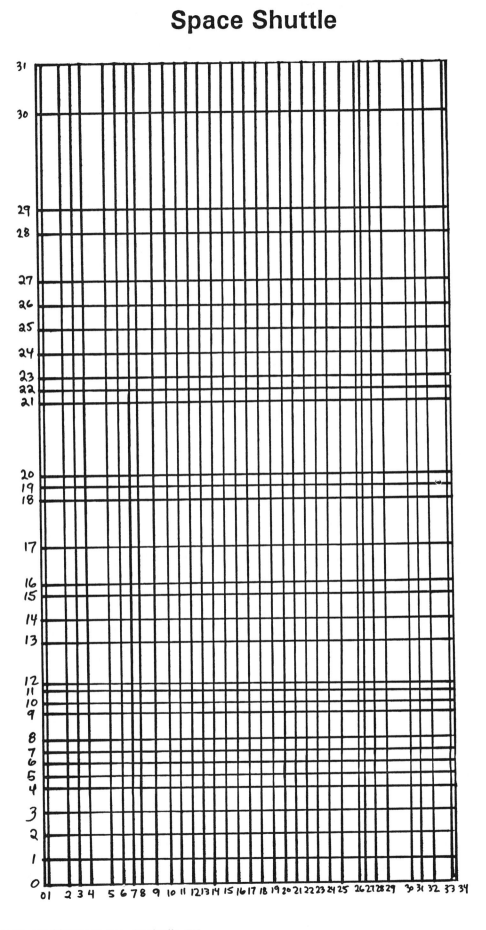

©1995 by Incentive Publications, Inc., Nashville, TN.

89

ANSWER KEY

1. Why did Mickey Mouse go into outer space? TO FIND PLUTO

2. Lines, Rays, and Line Segments. ANSWERS WILL VARY

3. Changing Line Segments.

3 points (3 lines)   5 points (10 lines)

4 points (6 lines)   6 points (15 lines)

4. How did Adam introduce himself to Eve, and it is also a palindrome? MADAM, I'M ADAM

5. What is the title of this picture?
    DIAPER FOR A PORCUPINE

6. What does the runner-up in a "Miss Universe" contest win?
    A CONSTELLATION PRIZE

7. Triangle Mania. 24

8. What's Dracula's favorite coffee? DECOFFINATED

9. Why should you beware of your computer? BECAUSE IT BYTES

10. Geobot. ANSWERS WILL VARY

11. What do you call an attractive angle? AN ACUTE ANGLE

12. Geometry In Our Environment. ANSWERS WILL VARY

14. Tangram Match-Up.

A sailboat

15. Symmetrical Design. ANSWERS WILL VARY

16. What kind of pliers do mathematicians use? MULTIPLIERS

17. Animalmania. (1) CICADA   (2) LIZARD

18. What geometric figure is like a runaway parrot?
    A POLYGON

19. How do you know Cyclops agree?
    BECAUSE THEY SEE EYE TO EYE

20. What did Snow White say when her photos were late coming?
    SOMEDAY MY PRINTS WILL COME

21. What did the acorn say when it grew up? GEOMETRY

22. If all the cars in the world were pink, what would you have? A PINK CARNATION

23. Who invented fractions? HENRY THE $\frac{1}{8}$

24. Why were Indians the first people in North America?
    THEY HAD RESERVATIONS

25. What happens when there's an explosion at a hotel?
    ROOMERS ARE FLYING

26. What time is it when you have a toothache?
    IT'S TOOTH-HURTY

29. Data Sheet - A Cube and a Rectangular Prism
    Cube - 1. 6   2. 12   3. 8   Volume = 125
    Rectangular Prism - 1. 6   2. 12   3. 8   Volume = 120

32. Data Sheet - A Pyramid and a Cylinder
    Square Pyramid - 1. 5   2. 8   3. 5
    Cylinder - 1. 2   2. 0   3. 0

33. Solid Figures. ANSWERS WILL VARY

37. Why is this a star for an eleven-year old? THE STAR HAS 11 POINTS

38. What bird prefers subfreezing temperatures and cannot fly? PENGUIN

39. Transforming a Triangle into a Chocolate Kiss

40. What animal is the most powerful winged predator of the night? OWL

41. Which present-day fish lived on earth during the time of the dinosaurs? SHARK

42. Design Distortion.

43. What flower is one of the first signs of spring? DAFFODIL

©1995 by Incentive Publications, Inc., Nashville, TN.

44. What weapon is used for defense on a gunboat? GUN TURRET

45. I am a three-horned dinosaur. TRICERATOPS

46. What animal has 40,000 muscles in its nose? ELEPHANT

47. United States Map.

48. What dinosaur used spikes to help it fight its enemies? STEGOSAURUS

49. A Pyramid of Cubes.

50. Chain.

51. Circles and Squares.

52. Something Familiar

53. What insect appears ferocious as a caterpillar? BUTTERFLY

54. What is the oldest living reptile? TURTLE

55. Heart.

56. Satellite.

MOON

A Nine-Pointed Star

57. What amphibian enjoys singing? FROG

58. What marsupial is known for its incredible speed and jumping power? KANGAROO

59-60. Geometric Extravaganza

61. Selling Apples
    1. McIntosh   2. 5, 5½, 8½   3. $168.00

62. Planets and Their Moons
    1. Pluto   2. Mercury, Venus   3. Saturn
    4. 17   5. 15   6. 2

63. Average Life Span of Some Familiar Animals
    1. Horse   2. Mouse   3. Dog, Sheep   4. Cow
    5. Squirrel, 4 years   6. Mouse, Rabbit
    7. Horse - 20 years
       Cow - 15 years
       Cat, Dog, Sheep - 12 years
       Pig, Squirrel - 10 years·
       Goat, Deer - 8 years
       Chipmunk - 6 years
       Rabbit - 5 years
       Mouse - 3 years

64. Our Missions to the Moon by the United States
    1. Apollo 13   2. Apollo 11   3. Apollo 17
    4. 2   5. 20 hours   6. About 55 hours
    7. About 295-300 hours   8. 4 years

©1995 by Incentive Publications, Inc., Nashville, TN.

65. Highest Mountains

1. Mt. Kilimanjaro 2. 20,000 ft. 3. Mt. Aconcagua
4. Mt. Everest 5. Australia 6. 4

66-67. Average Distance of Planets From the Sun

1. Mercury 2. c 3. b 4. c 5. a 6. a 7. b

68. Elevation and the Boiling Point of Water

1.c 2. c 3. a 4. decreases, increases
5. b 6. d

69. Creating Graphs. GRAPHS WILL VARY.

70-71. Graphing Project - Decision Making & Planning
ANSWERS WILL VARY

75. Geometric Puzzles with Tangrams

Geometric Puzzles with Tangrams Worksheet
76.

77. Octahedron Match 1. B 2. C 3. E 4. D 5. F 6. H 7. A 8. G

79. Remainder Math - Part I

Step 3.

C	0	1	2	3	4	5	6	7	8	9	10	11	12	13	14	15	16	17
R	5	6	7	8	9	10	11	12	13	14	15	16	17	0	1	2	3	4

Step 4.

Remainder Math - Part II, Circles 1-4
80.

Circle 1 Circle 2

Circle 3 Circle 4

81. Remainder Math - Part II, Circles 5-7

Circle 5 Circle 6

Circle 7

82. Remainder Math. ANSWERS WILL VARY

83-84. Proportional Drawing
DRAWING SHOULD BE FOUR TIMES LARGER

85-86. What bird of prey keeps the same
nest throughout its life? EAGLE

87-88. Space Shuttle.

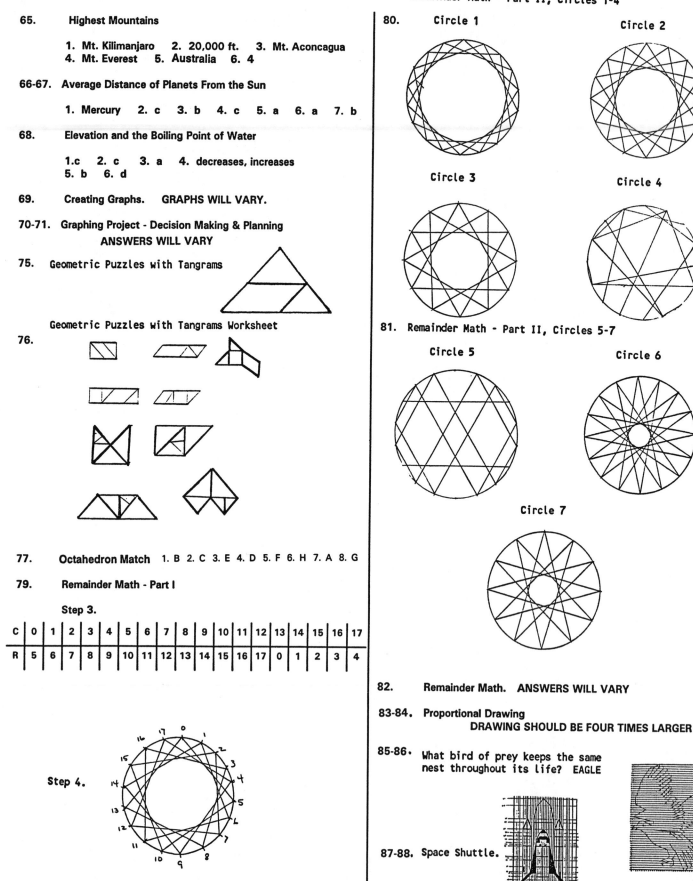

©1995 by Incentive Publications, Inc., Nashville, TN.